By the Word of Their Testimony

"And they overcame him because of the
blood of the Lamb and because of the
word of their testimony…"
Revelation 12:11

Take Heart! I have Overcome the World

Book 7

Erin Thiele

Cover Design by Dallas & Tara Thiele • NarrowRoad Publishing House

By the Word of Their Testimony

Take Heart! I have Overcome the World

By Erin Thiele

Published by:
NarrowRoad Publishing House
POB 830
Ozark, MO 65721 U.S.A.

The materials from Restore Ministries were written for the sole purpose of encouraging women. For more information, please take a moment to visit us at: **www.EncouragingWomen.org or www.RestsoreMinistries.net.**

Unless otherwise indicated, most Scripture verses are taken from the *New American Standard Bible* (NASB). Scripture quotations marked KJV are taken from the *King James Version* of the Bible, and Scripture quotations marked NIV are taken from the *New International Version.* Our ministry is not partial to any particular version of the Bible but **love** them all so that we are able to help every woman in any denomination who needs encouragement and who has a desire to gain greater intimacy with her Savior.

Library of Congress Control number: 2018913754
ISBN: 1-931800-42-1
ISBN 13: 978-1-931800-42-6

Contents

Introduction

Your Divine Appointment

"I was **crying** to the LORD with my voice,
And He **answered me** from His holy mountain"
—Psalm 3:4.

Have you been searching for marriage help? It's not by chance, nor is it by coincidence, that you are reading this book. God has heard your cry for help in your marriage dilemma. He predestined this DIVINE APPOINTMENT to give you the hope that you so desperately need right now!

If you have been told that your marriage is hopeless or that without your spouse's help your marriage cannot be restored, then this is the book you need. Read this over and over so you will begin to believe that God is MORE than able to restore ANY marriage, including YOURS!

We know and understand what you are going through since WE, and MANY others who have come to our ministry for help, have a restored marriage and family! No matter what others have told you, your marriage is NOT hopeless!! We KNOW, after twenty five years of ministry, that God is able to restore ANY marriage, even YOURS!

If you have been crying out to God for more help, someone who understands, then join our Internet Restoration Fellowship Online and you'll receive an ePartner (email partner) who will help you see your marriage through to restoration during your rebuilding phase of your journey. Since beginning this fellowship, we have seen more marriages restored on a regular basis than we ever thought possible!

So, if you are really serious in your desire to restore your marriage, then our fellowship is the answer. For more information or to join, go to our website RMIEW.com. We would love for you to be a part of our Restoration Fellowship!

Who are we and what are we hoping to do?

Restore Ministries helps those who have found themselves in a hopeless situation: couples whose spouse is in adultery, has left, has filed for divorce, or any other seemingly impossible marital situation. These broken people have often sought help, but everyone (many times even their pastors) have told them their marriage was hopeless. However, we not only believe that no marriage is hopeless – regardless of the circumstances—we know they aren't. That's why we offer hope, help and encouragement through our website, our Restoration Fellowship, and a variety of resources including a variety of newsletters to spiritual feed and uplift you daily!

In 2001, Restoration Fellowship was birthed to minister more effectively to the needs of those seriously seeking restoration. Within a year the fellowship grew to over 400 committed members and increases daily with members from all over the world.

Restore Ministries has never sought advertising or paid for placement in search engines but has instead grown by word of mouth. We also take no support from anyone but the individuals themselves who are seeking restoration so that we are never told we must comprise sharing His full truths. Though often ostracized by the established church, because of those who have cried out to God for help when their own church, pastor, family and friends who offered them no hope or support, we have given them hope and we have become an oasis in the desert for the desperate, the hurting, the rejected.

Often accused of being extreme, radical, out-of-balance or legalistic, the message in all our resources is founded firmly on the Word of God only, encouraging those seeking restoration to live the message that Jesus proclaimed, beginning with the familiar Beatitudes.

RMI teaches the good news of God's Word to bring healing to the brokenhearted, comfort to those in pain, and freedom to prisoners of despondency and sin through the truth of His Word, giving them the hope that is "against all hope" through the Power of Jesus Christ, the Mighty Counselor and Good Shepherd.

Our site and our resources minister to the hurting all over the world with the intent of creating a deeper and more intimate walk with the Lord that results in the hurting healed, the bound freed, the naked clothed, the lost saved and broken marriages restored. We minister to women from more than 15 countries including Switzerland, Hong Kong, New Zealand, Sweden,

Philippines, Brazil and Germany, with large followings in Australia, Canada, and Africa. Our books have been translated into Spanish, Portuguese, Tagalog (Filipino), Afrikaans, and French. Also Slovakian, Chinese, Russian, Italian and some Hindi.

Jesus said that you "will know them by their fruits" that's why this book and all our *By the Word of Their Testimony* books are filled with testimonies of hopeless marriages that were restored, marriages that give glory to God and to the Power of His Word. Our *WOTT* books are growing at such a phenomenal rate that we were once unable to keep up with getting them published. Now we have a full team devoted to keeping up.

If you have any doubt about the validly of our ministry, you won't after reading this and our other awesome books. Each will show you not only hopeless marriages that were restored, but more importantly, it will show you men and women who have been completely transformed into God-lovers and are now committed on-fire Christians, many of whom were saved through this ministry.

Below is a small sampling of the letters of gratitude that Restore Ministries has received. Please note when you read the letters that they give all the praise and glory to the Lord. This ministry was founded and continues to grow on the premise that "if He be lifted up, He will draw all men to Himself" and "the Lord will share His glory with no man."

"Let Another Praise You" Proverbs 27:2

Thank you for putting God's truth in an easy & accessible format. I realized I've been the problem in my marriage & I needed God to change me. I've grown closer to God & I see positive changes in my EH & marriage in such a short time. I have hope again. I'm encouraged daily.

My husband was living with OW. I didn't have any contact with my EH for months. I was depressed & suicidal.

Thank you, Lord, for leading me to RMI and showing me truth. Thank you for saving me from being a Pharisee. Thank you for changing my relationships for the better.

Dear friend, when your situation seems to be getting worse, praise God harder because God's power is stronger in our weakness. God is always working behind the scenes & working everything for your good. Never give up hope. Cry out to God & see Him move in your situation.

Keep trusting God. Allow God to work on you. Be still & see God move in your life.

~ Melissa in New Mexico Restored

I don't think that Thank You is enough to cover how much gratitude I feel! This course has been so very beneficial in my walk with the Lord! I have had principles taught and mostly reinforced to me. I know that He has anointed this ministry and led me here. I am so very very grateful that the course was given to me because it is so priceless!!

Thank you to the beautiful partners that sow into this ministry to make it possible for more and more marriages to be restored!

When I found you, I was and am still separated, but not legally. I was and still am believing God for a miracle in my marriage. These resources have confirmed many things about what I was doing wrong as a wife. They also helped me to be able to know I needed to let my husband know that I realize these things now and I don't blame him for wanting a divorce.

Thank You, Lord, for leading me to these wonderful resources. Please continue to bless and anoint them and all the ministers. Please help me to sow hope into other women to have restored marriages. Thank You for forgiving me. Thank you that you love marriage and you are teaching me to be the wife of my husband's dreams.

Dear Sister, I prayed for you before I began this note because that is the most POWERFUL gift I can give. I am pleased to be able to give you this gift because I know that my God shall supply all of my needs according to His riches in Glory. Please be sure to seek first His Kingdom and let everything else (husband and family) be added to you. I know that it is easier said than done but the Lord will honor your efforts when you put Him first. He will partner with you when you give him your YES. Keep your eyes on the Lord in all things and hide His Word in your heart so you will not Fear. NOTHING is IMPOSSIBLE for GOD!

When I first began here I had been on the Restoration Journey for a while and I was having a rather difficult time. I believe the Lord lead me here at just the right time. I think the main thing I learned is to Trust in the Lord with all your heart as in Proverb 3:5-6.

~ Rachel in Ontario Restored

I want to thank the partners of RMI for whom I had the privilege of taking the courses: RYM, Renew, Wise Woman and all the Abundant Life series FREE to me! And now I am just beginning the course of Living the Abundant Life today and can already see the good fruits that it has brought into my life—each of these courses and lessons learned!

I am deeply grateful to God for bringing me to this ministry and with you, dear partners, by faithfully tithing as this has given so many of us the opportunity to know the truth and be free!! God bless each of your lives greatly for your loyalty and for donating to RMI so faithfully.

My relationship with my Beloved HH has grown and I'm being restored daily, which is quite exciting! Pain and tears are gone and today, thanks to how you've blessed me, there is a smile on my face, because knowing Him as my HH has been the best experience of my life, and would not have been possible without your donations, thousand and thousand of thanks!!

I thank God for leading me to this material, like the first book "How God can and will restore your marriage" it removed the blindfolds, helped me see my situation through the eyes of God, I could understand my situation and it definitely gave me hope, and the guidelines and principles that would help me find the restoration, read daily devotional and corresponding lesson of the book and fill out the forms of "what I learned" allowed me to get closer, pour out my heart to Him and know better my HH, who has become my all and all!!!.

After following the principles, I've seen the changes in me and in my marriage. I know that God continues to work on both, and that in His time, restoration will continue to come, for now, I focus on Him and enjoy this time with my HH even more than before restoration!

Dear bride, follow each course and follow the instructions given to you along each, obedience has its rewards. Gradually you will see how He is working and is responding to your prayers, you will see how the crying decreases and joy returns back to your life in a supernatural way, you will see how the peace that surpasses all understanding envelops you even in situations that your eyes see could be disastrous. He will embrace you every moment!!! You'll fall in love with Him and you'll feel full and satisfied!

Thank you, dear partners, for the book "By the word of their testimony" definitely encouraged me throughout my journey, reading testimonials everyday helped me realize that my marriage had hope that my testimony someday will be one of those in your books! That's why I'll be helping to distribute paperback books to poor Latin-speaking countries.

Before finding this Ministry I had sought help many and some relatives of my EH, I prayed but did not know my HH at all actually. All I did on the advice of (well-meaning) pastors and my family made matters much worse. It turned my EH against me, I had no peace, was bitter, sad, crying all the time, did not eat and no longer I wanted to live. With these attitudes, my home was nothing but a disaster and a place where no one wanted to be.

That's when my HH heard my cry and gave me a "Hope at Last"! I fill out the questionnaire and start reading the book of RYM through, then I understood and I could see all my mistakes, I realized I'd definitely contributed a lot in the destruction of my marriage! But glory to God, His truth set me free!!

My Love!! Like every day I thank You again for guiding me to the truth, thank You that through these resources I could know the truth, experience this love towards You and have the revelation of Your love for me, which was what made the difference in wanting to live. I am eternally grateful to You my love, because I have more than I deserve, having You has been the best thing that ever happened to me! Now I know You, Your love has filled my heart and with that I I gained life! Thanks, my Love!!

~ Natty in Denmark Restored

We put this book and all our *Word of Their Testimony* books together because we believe that as you spend some time reading these incredible and awesome testimonies of seemingly hopeless marriages that were miraculously restored, you will be encouraged and know without a doubt...

NOTHING IS IMPOSSIBLE WITH GOD!!

Nothing is Impossible
with God!

"Looking at them, Jesus said,
'With people it is impossible,
but not with God;
for all things are possible with God.'"
Mark 10:27

*"And they overcame him because of the blood of the Lamb and because of the **word of THEIR testimony**, and they did not love their life even to death." Rev. 12:11.*

The following testimonies are filled with miracles of men and women who took God at His Word and believed that "nothing was impossible with God!" Those who have had the miracle of a restored marriage have several things in common. All "delighted themselves in the Lord" and He gave them "the desires of their heart." All of them "hoped against hope" when their situation seemed hopeless.

All of them "fought the good fight" and "finished their course." All of them were determined "not to be overcome with evil" but instead to "overcome evil with good." All were willing to "bless their enemies" and to pray for them that "despitefully used and persecuted them." All "turned the other cheek" and "walked the extra mile." All realized that it was "God who removed lover and friend far from" them and it was God who "made them a loathing" to their spouse. All of them understood and believed that it is NOT the will of man (or woman) but the "will of God" who can "turn the heart" whichever way He chooses.

All refused to fight in "the flesh" but chose to battle "in the spirit." None were concerned to protect themselves, but trusted themselves "to Him who judges righteously." All of their trust was "in the Lord" because their trust was "the Lord." All released their attorneys (if that was part of their testing)

since they "would rather be wronged or defrauded." All of them "got out of the way of wickedness" and "let the unbeliever leave" since they "were called to peace." All refused to do "evil for evil or insult for insult." All loved their spouse who may have been unfaithful because they knew that "love never fails."

This is the same journey that the Lord took me on back in 1989. That year I made a promise to God that if He would restore my marriage to my husband, I would devote my life to telling others about Him and His desire and ability to restore ANY marriage no matter what the circumstances. The Lord was faithful and restored my marriage, suddenly, two years later after a divorce. (Yes! AFTER a divorce!) Now I faithfully, with the Lord's continued help, love, support, and guidance, spread the GOOD news that nothing—NOT A THING—is impossible with God!

It is important to know that our ministry was FOUNDED to help all those who were told by pastors and Christian friends that their situations were HOPELESS. Those who come to us for hope are facing a spouse who is deep in adultery, who has moved out (often in with the other man or woman who committed adultery with), who has already filed for divorce or whose divorce has gone through. 99% of those who come, come alone for help since their spouse is not interested in saving their marriage, but is desperately trying to get out. Over 95% claim that they are Christians and most are married to Christians.

Over half are in some type of Christian service and many of the men who are involved with other woman are pastors who have left not only their wife and children, but their church as well.

If you, or if someone you know, is facing devastation in their marriage, there is hope. Read these awesome testimonies that prove that God is MORE than able to restore ANY marriage—even YOURS!

Chapter 1

Whitley

"Better is a dry morsel
and quietness
with it than a house full of feasting
with strife"
—Proverbs 17:1

"Discover your HH. Fall in Love. Make Him number One"

Whitley, how did your restoration actually begin?

Well, it all started when my son got sick and I took him to the pediatrician. My son's pediatrician said that if it did not improve to inform him. My son did not improve so I sent him a text message asking him what I could do. From there every day I received a message from him asking if my son had improved and soon we became friends. He began to compliment me on my wonderful mothering, but when that happened, I tried to change the because I was uncomfortable. It wasn't planned, when we became friends, but at the time, I didn't see the harm being friendly with my son's pediatrician because it was easier if he had a problem.

My mistake was being too innocent or maybe stupid, because I simply had not realized what was happening. In one of our conversations the doctor said that he liked to write poetry and that's actually is my passion. I'm a teacher and I have written a lot of poetry myself, but nobody ever cared. So, when this man actually wanted to read what I wrote I got really excited. That day, even though I had lots, I sent him just two to read.

Of course, I was finding it strange having received so many compliments from him, it seemed he was texting me every day with a new topic to discuss but I just enjoyed the attention. So, just to be sure it was okay, I decided to copy part of the conversation and I emailed to a friend.

Then one day, I was trying to help a friend who was also having problems in her marriage and asked my husband to send her an email for me. My account was open because I had nothing to hide. That's when he saw all the pediatrician's messages that I'd emailed my friend that I'd copied from my phone. He was furious. That day he packed a bag and he left home for 4 days. When he returned he had separation papers for me to sign— even though nothing happened.

How did God change your situation Whitley as you sought Him wholeheartedly?

I have been a Christian since I was 19 but I had fallen away. Many times, I would not go to church in order to stay home with my husband to make him happy. Little did I know that having this attitude, not just about church, but putting him first above everything— proved I was unintentionally putting my husband in first place. When everything happened, and my husband said he wanted a separation, I finally turned to God for help. I had the book *How God Can and Will Restore Your Marriage* but had not read yet. I don't remember who gave it to me, or why, but there it sat.

Desperately I searched for a church close to home but when I read *HopeAtLast.com*, I knew that it wasn't a church I needed. It was Him I needed. From there I made the Lord my number one priority. I started reading the RYM book and taking notes. I read everything that could to keep me close to God. I began succeeding in many things in my life, moving forward, one day at a time. I remember that my husband spent four days in our country house and when he came back he had already made the decision to divorce me. I told him that I thanked God for going through this nightmare because only then did I realize that nothing could take the place of the Lord in my life.

What principles, from God's Word (or through our resources), Whitley, did the Lord teach you during this trial?

I asked God for wisdom and patience, but the basic principle was to overcome evil with good and winning my husband without a word. Keeping silent. My husband made it a point to try to humiliate me every chance he got, he told me horrible things, played jokes on me, posted things on social media, but each time He said to say nothing, do nothing. God helped me get through it. Silence is the most powerful weapon we have and what will win most battles. To all of you who are hoping for restoration, wait solely and exclusively on the Lord. Put all your hope in Him.

Dear Brides, I do encourage you to read *Finding the Abundant Life* especially "Your Best Protection." All of us ladies are longing for protection, we have this written in our DNAs, so why not take some time to really think about an innate basic need for every woman? We know what our Savior did for us, and what He is able to do if we Trust Him, otherwise, we may live our lives as unfortunate and needy women while we have it all taken care already by our HH. With all my heart, I encourage you to read about your best protection ever - your BRIDEGROOM.

As I've said, I highly recommend the course, this *Finding the Abundant Life* book!!! My faith has been improved so much more than anything I've read, and my whole life has been improved by the principles that are taught.

He does have a great life for us all, for all His BRIDES. Sometimes HE IS going to deliver us from the evil, but other times we are going to face the evil, so we need to learn to be loving towards the ones that are trying to harm to us. As soon as we learn to listen to HIM, and to quiet down in HIS arms enjoying HIS companionship, it will be the speed to find peace for our souls and genuine joy.

Speaking simplistically, summarizing everything—all we need is the assurance that He is with us, HE LOVES us and takes good care of us. That's what HE DOES, that's HIS nature, HE IS OUR HUSBAND.

As soon as we discovered that we are just fine in the exact situation that we are in, the position we are because HE is the One who will continue orchestrating all things for our good, because we love Him and because HE DOES have a plan for our lives.

Through this book, we are guided to forgive others, expect less from people that surround us, to forgive ourselves, to be glad about our waiting time, to be grateful about every detail of our journey. Michele helps us understand this great TRUTH with this book. She helps all of us Brides, to find our abundant life that is HIDDEN IN OUR BRIDEGROOM.

In the end, time doesn't matter anymore, once we are delighting ourselves with our BELOVED. The scenario doesn't matter, HE IS GOING to be there with us, and we can trust HIM, HE always takes great care of HIS BRIDES. Please learn how to enjoy the BEST, HIS COMPANIONSHIP IS THE BEST!!!

An abundant life? I already have it, He gave it to me long before my restoration, and I do belong to HIM, HE is my abundant life!!!

Whitley, what was the "turning point" of your restoration?

The turning point was from the beginning when I made it clear that I would no longer leave my first Love. I told myself, told God, told my HH that He was first, but I'd always spoken about my EH constantly. My feelings for him were evident and where he was in my life, number one and an idol. Once I TRULY was faithful to my HH, the most amazing things happened. First, no more pain. No matter what I heard or didn't hear regarding my EH, it didn't affect me one bit. What a MIRACLE yet it's everything RMI tells us, Erin says, and each RMT I read says. But I just didn't get it and I only fooled myself that I'd let go and my HH was first until then.

The next thing is that my EH feelings for me CHANGED. This happened before, but each time before, I'd quickly make him and my marriage my idol again, only to have my EH turn away and reject me again. But once I didn't care, once my HH was truly MY FIRST LOVE, I just didn't care when my EH was nice to me. This caused him to begin pursuing me! Another miracle but again what this ministry has told me from DAY ONE.

Tell us HOW it happened Whitley? Did your husband just walk in the front door? Whitley, did you suspect or could you tell you were close to being restored?

How it happened started when I got pregnant two months into my RJ. Though he'd filed for divorce, it was clear he had feelings for me. So, since we were still married, and based on what I learned from RMI, I was submissive to his advances. Yet, rather than be my miracle, my pregnancy was awful. My EH became horribly distant, but I did not ask for anything: no support, no affection. To my EH it was as if I was not pregnant.

Once my son was born and he started to talk more to me, we began to have a good relationship, but there was still a great chasm between us. It was clear he wasn't fully in, so I asked if He would show me restoration was taking place. My EH was still not wear the wedding ring and it bothered my family a lot. One day after hearing from my family how shameful this was, I was telling God that the sign that my marriage was being restored was when he put the ring back on. That would be the sign this was His will.

Then one day as I was leaving the bathroom and he came in from the other room saying he had thought I deserved better and I saw he had his ring back on. In all, my journey lasted a year, but the TRUTHS and my TRANSFORMATION will last for a LIFETIME.

Would you recommend any of our resource in particular that helped you Whitley?

First I would recommend the book *How God Can and Will Restore Your Marriage* and reading the *Encourager* and of course, the online courses offered by RMI. It is very important to always remain close to everything that leads you to the Lord and this ministry does that. Discovering your *HH* and the *Finding the Abundant Life Course* is when your life will really change.

Also, if you sense you're not being blessed and there's something stopping it, I'd look at tithing to your storehouse. This is when my miracles stopped being stolen the moment they happened. Read how to *surrender and trust* Him and where you're spiritually fed.

Would you be interested in helping encourage other women Whitley?

Yes

Either way Whitley, what kind of encouragement would you like to leave women with, in conclusion?

Give your heart completely to HIM. Allow yourself to be broken, then SURRENDER yourself to Him. Ask for forgiveness for your sins. Speak to HIM always as if it were your last prayer. Trust. Believe His promises. Ask for WISDOM. Say NOTHING. Quietness is your best weapon. Seek God more and more. He will hear you. Discover your HH. Fall in Love. Make Him number One. I do not know how long your fight will last but be sure that God gives you Victory. Do not rush, it's all in God's timing, not yours. Mine lasted a year, yours could last more or less. God knows what each of us has to go through in order to change. Find your HH early on so you can enjoy your journey.

Chapter 2

Valery

"No good deed will He withhold
to those who walk uprightly."
—Psalm 84:11

"I was Pregnant- He wasn't the Father"

Valery, how did your restoration actually begin?

My restoration journey actually began just a couple of months shy of 2 years ago. Both my husband and I committed adultery in our marriage several years back. I was the first to stray, then my husband retaliated against me, and got involved with the OW. During this time my husband left to another state to work, and I just followed him. I quit my job, got a new job, and tried doing everything I could think of to keep him at my side. He was so cold and distant. That was the most heart-wrenching time of my life, I felt so betrayed.

At the time I was so naive, not knowing that the other woman was actually still seeing him. They would travel the 4-hour drive, to see one another. When I found out, I confronted him and went into a rage. He told me that I could stay or go, but he would continue doing what he wanted.

At the time I was pregnant with my son. I didn't tell him he wasn't the father. I ran to God, not knowing where to turn, after not being able to find answers or peace amongst my family. Two months before giving birth to my son, I found out that the OW was pregnant too. I was devastated, but by the Grace of God, somehow I got through this. After my son was born, I was too busy for God and stopped praying.

Eventually, my husband left the OW, but we now had to deal with his daughter, with the OW.

Fast forward to two years ago. I thought we had forgiven each other, but my husband began distancing himself. I thought he may be involved with someone, but couldn't prove anything. He began blaming me for everything, including his involvement with the OW! He turned cold and refused to go anywhere with me.

Recently he was summoned to go to court for child support, which caused more strain in my marriage. My husband started coming and going, as he pleased. He also started drinking more. It was during this time that I began searching online for prayers, about pleading the blood of Jesus over my marriage, which led me to your website.

How did God change your situation Valery as you sought Him wholeheartedly?

Coming here is when everything changed. God helped me learn to trust Him, to lean on His understanding, not my own. I was so scared and afraid to trust Him, at first. I cried out to Him, mainly to restore my marriage, but at the same time, I was still trying to cling to my own ways. I continually read my bible, hoping and praying for God to change my husband, not knowing it was I, who needed to change.

After finding your site, I ended up finding out how prideful and contentious I really was. I repented of the ways I treated my husband. The courses and testimonies have really helped me see how wrong my thinking was. Not only was I focusing on his sin, but I was also dealing with feelings of guilt and shame as a result of my own sin.

What principles, from God's Word (or through our resources), Valery, did the Lord teach you during this trial?

Forgiveness. After finding this site, I started to question myself about truly forgiving and started praying for all of the people that have hurt me, letting go of the wrong they'd done to me.

I didn't trust what the world said about divorce or know what God's word was, but I knew in my heart that divorce wasn't for me. Through this site, I've discovered the knowledge of His promises, to stand on.

What were the most difficult times that God helped you through Valery?

I was determined to keep God in my heart and stay in my home, even when I felt that I was losing hope. I admit there were thoughts about me just up and leaving, but I would cast them down, and kept moving forward on my journey. I felt a lot of fear but knew that God didn't give me a spirit of fear, but of peace, love, and a sound mind. PTL!

Valery, what was the "turning point" of your restoration?

It was actually unexpected, while my husband was gone after his grandmother died, he had no contact with me. He would call my children, but wouldn't ask to speak to me. I just let go and kept meditating on letting God restore.

Dear Brides, O taste and see How good our Beloved is. He wanted to remind you that He has your situation in total control! He knows the plans that He has for you, and what you are currently experiencing is uniquely designed for you so that you may experience His plans for hope, a future, and prosperity in Him. I want to encourage you to stop resisting and take refuge in our Almighty who is at work, actively ensuring that soon, at the "appointed time" when you are ready to begin to walk in the Abundant Live He is calling You to lead, then you too will be restored. I love you and will continue to pray for you all :)

Tell us HOW it happened Valery? Did your husband just walk in the front door? Valery, did you suspect or could you tell you were close to being restored?

He came home on a Saturday, his flight came in late, and his friend picked him up. I didn't actually see him until Sunday, the next evening, after I was off work. He went back to his other house, that night, and stayed until Monday. On Tuesday he said he would be spending the night with "his" son. I was happy, but I told myself not to get my hopes up, to trust Him. I was ready to let him leave again if he chose to. I had recently watched Erin's, Be Encouraged videos, and in week 2, of the courses, I felt somewhat prepared for whatever happened. During the night, he came to my bed, and we were intimate. I didn't discourage him, or say anything, as if nothing had ever happened. He never left and it's been 10 months. Now we spend time with my son and his daughter who many think are twins.

Dear brides, read the testimonies and praise reports to renew your mind and see what the Lord has done in the lives of all women who trusted Him even when all seems to be so wrong and impossible. You will see that NONE was alone or ashamed because He is always faithful. What He did for them, He will do for you if you trust Him your life and decisions. This is a life journey and every step He takes you is to refine and make you a better bride, so you can enjoy your abundant life the way He perfectly planned.

Did you suspect or could you tell you were close to being restored?

I didn't suspect anything at all. God turned his heart at His appointed time! Glory to God!

Would you recommend any of our resource in particular that helped you Valery?

How God Can and Will Restore Your Marriage. And now I recommend *Finding the Abundant Life Course.* It is an excellent book to read. It is straight from the Lord's Word. It will not steer you wrong. The principles will help you in a favorable way. If it worked for these women and worked for me, it will work for you too. God is not a respecter of persons.

Do you have favorite Bible verses, Valery, that you would like to pass on to women reading your Testimonies? Promises that He gave you?

"What God has joined together, let no man tear asunder." Matthew 19:6

"No good deed will He withhold to those who walk uprightly." Psalm 84:11

"Husbands should love their wives as they love their own bodies." Ephesians 5:28

"Husbands should love their wives, as Christ loved the church, and gave himself up for her." Ephesians 5:25

"For your Husband is your Maker, Whose name is the Lord of hosts; And your Redeemer is the Holy One of Israel, Who is called the God of all the earth. For the Lord has called you, Like a wife forsaken and grieved in spirit, Even like a wife of one's youth when she is rejected,' Says your God"–Isaiah 54:4-6

Would you be interested in helping encourage other women Valery?

Yes

Either way Valery, what kind of encouragement would you like to leave women with, in conclusion?

Don't allow the world to persuade you to give up on your marriage, that's the easy way out, anybody can do that. It takes a courageous woman, to stay, with God's help, and see your marriage restored. With God, all things are possible! All the praise and glory. Thank you, Erin, and everyone working for this ministry. God bless you all!

Dear Brides, the Lord loves you with an everlasting love. His is waiting for you. All he requires is for us to follow his commandments. To obey, to listen, to all those that are in authority over us. We will gain favor with the Lord if we do this.

Chapter 3

Janelle

"Trust in the Lord with all your heart
and lean not on your own understanding;
in all your ways submit to him,
and he will make your paths straight."
—Proverbs 3:5

"EH Confessed OW was Expecting his Child"

Janelle, how did your restoration actually begin?

My EH never wanted to leave his home but I kicked him out several times. I would leave the house and he would never kick me out. I was so full of rage, rebellion, jealousy, you name it—everything but the Fruit of the Spirit. A friend going through a separation sent me a Spanish audio of a book *How God Can and Will Restore Your Marriage.* I listened and re-listened to it several times and I knew I wanted more. It automatically touched my heart and convicted me. I needed to read the book in English and I ordered it. Although I am not a reader I devoured this book within days!

When I filled out the Marriage Evaluation Questionnaire and it asked me to tell about my situation and why I had come to your ministry for help, I said:

I NEED encouragement. I had my suspicious that may husband had another woman about two years ago. I did everything wrong! I was jealous, bitter, vengeance, angry. I kicked him out several times, I also left the house several times. I spoke to everyone about our situation desperately looking for comfort/solution, that just made everything worse and pushed him more into the ow's arms. I finally got a hold of your How God Can and Will Restore My Marriage and I finally am beginning to see my situation turn a little but also I am changing.

God has shown me so much of my errors/sins through your book. In September, around the same time I receive your book, my husband told me the ow is pregnant with his child. Because of my previous reactions, he believed I would again throw him out but since I had started reading the book and was starting to change I didn't. But he had already got an apartment, thinking I would explode in anger and kick him out again. He saw I didn't and we spoke a lot about our situation. He said he needed to be alone to think things and left. This time did not tell him to leave. He told me he needed about 2 months to think things. I was kind and I told him I wanted to change my contentious ways and I think he did see a change.

He "lived" in his apartment around 2 weeks and told me he was coming back. This time I did not tell him to leave, to stay, or to come back. He did everything on his own. He says that he feels bad for the ow because she is only 20 years old, is an illegal, is alone in this country, has no one in this city and she was also a victim of hurricane Harvey and has no place to live.

He has told me he doesn't love her and he wants his marriage and loves me but knows I will not forgive him. I have apologized several times for my ways and I am changing. He stays the night in his apartment 1 or 2 days out of the week. He says he likes to go to be alone and think about things. He still comes home late like he would before around 12-2 AM during the week.

Every time he comes home late or doesn't come home, I get very discouraged and I have a real mental problem, which I know is the enemy trying to discourage me. I have apologized to our families for getting them involved. I have the read the book 2 times and have now purchased and am reading A Wise Woman. I don't know if I shouldn't have let him in so fast and still have my doubts if he still is involved with the ow, not just as a responsible man but emotional/physically involved with her. We have been married for 17 years.

Before coming here I'd searched and found other Marriage Ministry sites. I'd had some Personal Counseling. I'd spoken to my pastor. I'd shared my situation with my family. I'd shared my situation with my husband's family. I'd shared my situation with friends/neighbors. I'd shared my situation with Coworkers.

I know my Lord is able to do anything and everything but many times I do feel defeated and discouraged, as if I want to give up and I can't go on. I want to be obedient to God and His Word. I love my husband, my family (we have 2 kids a 14-year-old and an 11-year-old) I want to give my kids an example what a real Christian marriage should be and remain married.

Father I humbly come to you to give you all the glory and praise. I ask that you give me strength to do Your will and not mine. My flesh tells me to give up on my marriage and give up on my husband, but Your Word says to pick up my cross and Your yoke is easy. Please give me the strength to go on and give me strength to keep calm and kind. I want to reflect You in my life. Please Father help my husband in his temptation. Clear his mind and take the blinders off his eyes. Give him strength to do that right thing. Place in him a fresh love for You, his marriage and family. Thank you, Lord, for everything that you do. In Jesus' name, Amen.

While my Lord was changing me little by little, a lot of stuff was still going on with my EH. One day I saw my EH and the OW together but even then, he still denied it but I was so new in my RJ and I had a long way to go. That means I was still contentious and made him admit it, that they had a thing. My Lord gave me the strength to endure that, but I was still in a lot of pain and very hurt.

A couple of days later my EH confessed that the OW was expecting his child and that he had a gotten an apartment because he knew I was going to overreact and go crazy. Before I heard the audios, I had even become violent, screaming and cursing, something that I would never have done before. But He is so good, I didn't react with violence or anger. I was extremely calm but at the same time extremely hurt and in so much pain! The verse that made me sorrowful to the point of true repentance and salvation (2 Corinthians 7:9-10) really plays in my mind, explaining the sorrow I felt. I was in my RJ and just starting with your ministry when this all happened.

A couple days later he moved out and into his apartment. I stood out of his way and I was amazed at the peace my Lord gave me. But I still had a lot to learn and my journey was just beginning.

How did God change your situation Janelle as you sought Him wholeheartedly?

I started praying and seeking Him every morning and during the day. Writing the verses down in a spiral notebook from the RYM book. My EH always kept in touch and would come by every day and I truly thought he would be gone for at least a year. My journey was slow because of me removing things from my life and Him changing me. He patiently helped me over *hurdles* that I so many times didn't want to jump over. He would give me the strength and peace to endure.

What principles, from God's Word (or through our resources), Janelle, did the Lord teach you during this trial?

So many principles I have been learning through your resources. But during this trial, He taught me that I needed to trust Him and to stop being contentious. To not say a word. Writing down scriptures onto my 3X5 cards helped so much. Also tithing and becoming a *partner*. I love how your ministry team encouraged me and I wanted other women to get the same encouragement.

May I say how grateful and thankful I am for the partners' gift for these courses! I took my time on each course and made sure I understood everything that was being given. I had my spiritual breakthrough at the end of your Course 2! PTL! I don't want what I have to ever end, these courses are amazing. I learn each day more and more. It challenged me to get over *hurdles* that I didn't want to get over and ladies once I took those leaps of faith, it was like weights coming off my shoulders. When I thought any lesson really didn't pertain to me, that's when my Lord would speak to me even more. I can't wait to start the new course, course 3, that is to follow and learn more to renew my mind, heal me more and have more breakthroughs! :) THANK YOU, LADIES!

When I found your ministry, I was so desperate for the Truth. I went to different churches, friends, family and just once to counseling and nothing and no one could truly help me. My EH of 17 years was not acting right and hiding and using his phone a lot. He was disappearing a lot. I was a Pharisee making myself the innocent victim. I was so rebellious, bitter, arrogant, prideful, grumpy and contentious. Since the beginning of my journey, God told me this was a spiritual battle. I was advised by many to leave him, divorce him and find myself another man. I would feel deep inside that this was not the way to go. Thank You my Lord for protecting me. I would always answer them that I wanted to do it God's way.

We had a broken, doomed marriage from the beginning, built on a very sandy foundation that I tried for years to fix on my own, yet things were getting worse. A friend going through the same situation led me to your ministry by giving me some audios of the book How God Can and Will Restore but in Spanish. As soon as I heard it, it started speaking to me and convicting me of everything. I heard and re-listened to these audios over and over. I had to purchase the book in English, so I did.

As I said, I am not a reader and how I engulfed the book within days is a testament to its power. And the changes I made were drastic but still I had a way to go. I became someone unknown to me. I was extremely jealous and had become violent and screaming and cursing. But as soon as I heard the audios, again as I said, I let go of those ways and have become much calmer. While this was happening within me I saw my EH and the OW together. He always denied it and when I saw them he still denied it, but I was still contentious and made him tell me. He then confessed to me a couple days later that she was expecting a child and that he had gotten an apartment because he knew I was going to explode on him and everything.

Well, I didn't! But that totally broke me, and I can totally relate to the verse that says I was made sorrowful to point of true repentance and salvation. I needed more than the book and I finally found your website. Oh, what a blessing it has been. I started my courses in November and how much my Lord has changed me in just 5 months— it has truly been an amazing journey.

I never thought I could pray the way I am. I never thought I would read as much as I am today. I never thought I would have the peace and faith that I have today! When my EH left to his apartment I thought it was over for sure and he wouldn't be back for at least a year. But I got out of his way and let him leave without fighting or screaming or manipulating. He was gone for 6 days and my Lord turned his heart and brought him back home. But I was not ready, I was just in the beginning of my journey crawling, not even baby steps.

My trials are even tougher than ever, but I have your resources that have helped me so much in my RJ. When I first started I thought this was all about restoring my marriage and now I see that He is restoring my relationship with Him, which is the most important. He is lovingly, patiently, kindly removing, healing, peeling so many things out of my life that I didn't even know needed fixing. I still have a way to go in my journey and my EH is still not saved. Even though my marriage isn't what it's supposed to be, I know He is faithful and I praise Him for what He has promised He'll finish. I am forever grateful for your ministry and for my Lord. THANK YOU!

THANK YOU, MY BELOVED LORD, for hearing my cry for help and leading me to this ministry. Thank you for Your Truths and Word that truly set me free. Thank You for Your promises. I praise You for the beautiful work You do in our lives. I am so grateful for You and all that You do.

Ladies, I know the pain and the hopelessness you feel. Do not believe those lies. Take it one day at a time and open your heart to our beloved Lord. He has been waiting for you. He is able to transform that pain to joy, and those worries to peace. Just give Him a chance, what do you have to lose? This ministry is a blessing, it has been for me. It has helped me to find true peace and it has set me free of so many lies. The ministers will lead you in the right direction, which is directly to Him, our beloved Heavenly Husband!

Ladies have faith that our Lord is able to do the impossible. I know you are hurting and the pain is overwhelming, I know I've been there! Know this that if you open your heart and obey Him, He will help you get through this. Just take it day by day and by the time you know it you will be stronger, and you won't feel the pain anymore. Have faith in Him. He loves you and He will never let you down.

What were the most difficult times that God helped you through Janelle?

There were so many, but the main ones were when I saw them together and when I found out the OW was pregnant. Yet He gave me peace and strength even though I felt my heart was being torn into pieces. I have two kids; a teenager and a preteen, and He would give me the strength and peace they needed. I needed to function and do our daily school tasks. He also helped me to keep my mouth shut and allow my EH to confess his new child to our family and kids. I used to be so contentious and confess his sins to everyone, HUGE MISTAKE, which I am so shameful for ever doing.

Janelle, what was the "turning point" of your restoration?

Two or three days after my EH left he told me he was coming home soon. I didn't believe him but just kept seeking God. I wasn't ready but had the resources now that are helping me change. I still had a long way to go and sometimes wonder why He does things the ways He does things. So, He answers me with that His ways are not my ways and my thoughts are not His thoughts.

I feel like I didn't have my turning point until later on, much later on, in my restoration. One month ago, I had my spiritual breakthrough. A month ago, I felt like I finally started to truly let go of so many things, not only my EH but many other things and when I truly started embracing my Lord as my HH.

Tell us HOW it happened Janelle? Did your husband just walk in the front door? Janelle, did you suspect or could you tell you were close to being restored?

My EH came home 6 days after he left. And just like Erin says in one of her lessons, I didn't think or imagine it happening that way. He just brought his things back into the garage. Not even inside the house. I believe he was testing me to see how it would go. I was very proud before and in my past state of mind I would have left his clothes and belongings in the garage and let him bring them in himself. However, I felt the Holy Spirit lead me to get all his stuff and put everything back in their rightful place. And that changed everything.

The lessons are on point, the trials are coming even more now because the enemy is still trying to destroy us. But I use this to keep pressing closer to HH, this is my goal. Our journey is still in the process and I know He is still not done with us.

Did you suspect or could you tell you were close to being restored Janelle?

No, not at all! I truly thought my EH was going to be gone for months, maybe years. I didn't think he would come home so fast. It has taken me a long time to do this but through a lesson, my Lord brought it to my attention that I never submitted a PR for my restoration. Like Erin said in the lesson, I didn't "feel" like I was restored. The enemy had me so blinded and didn't want me to praise my Lord for what He has done! But thank you, Erin, for these lessons and helping us be set free from the lies and schemes of the enemy!

Would you recommend any of our resource in particular that helped you Janelle?

Yes, I recommend it ALL. The book *How God Can and Will Restore Your Marriage, A Wise Woman* that I'm currently reading. The *devotionals*. EVERYTHING you can get your hands on is such a blessing! I especially encourage you to do the *RRR online courses*. Those have been what truly helped me. I was so blinded when I first began I could barely praise my Lord! But each day doing the journal I have to praise Him, and I am so thankful for that. It truly renewed and changed my mind! It helped me each day and is teaching me each day new things and all with scriptures to back it up.

Do you have favorite Bible verses, Janelle, that you would like to pass on to women reading your Testimonies? Promises that He gave you?

Yes, Proverbs 3:5-7 "Trust in the Lord with all your heart and do not lean on your own understanding. In all your ways acknowledge Him, and He will make your paths straight. Do not be wise in your own eyes; fear the Lord and turn away from evil."

This verse I am still using. Every time I would see and hear things that were not good news I would say this scripture and tell myself I will not lean on my own understanding, but I will trust in my Lord.

Would you be interested in helping encourage other women Janelle?

YES!

Either way Janelle, what kind of encouragement would you like to leave women with, in conclusion?

Please DON'T give up. He is faithful, He knows what He is doing. He will never let you down. Focus on Him, remain in His Word, focus on His promises.

DON'T believe the lies and DON'T entertain the enemy in your mind. Place your hope on Him. Praise Him at all times and in all the ways you can.

Be content, that will help you change your mindset. Follow and obey and you will see the wonders and blessing He has for you.

DON'T allow your pain and hurt to swallow you up. Go to Him, it's ok to cry to Him and give Him your pain, He is able and capable to bring you out of it.

My Restoration Journey Continues

EH Asked Me to Help Him Sell the OW Car!?!

My EH is a musician, what started as a hobby turned into what I have referred to as his god. I have never liked my EH being a musician, I knew it was too much temptation and I didn't know my Beloved as I do now. My faith was very weak. I would always pray to Him to remove my EH from that music world. This was in 2016. In 2017 I finally let it go and gave it to God. I remember telling God, I know You are able to remove him from that world and I don't know why you haven't, but I will trust in You. And I truly let it go.

My EH would go play on weekends, practice during the weekdays and I would be at peace with God knowing it was on his time.

Today my EH told me he is sick and tired of that music world and wanted out! Praise the LORD! I wanted to shout HALLELUJAH! But I contained my emotions and MY MOUTH. He told me that the group he was in told him they didn't want him any longer. I really didn't like the group too much, they knew too much of our personal lives and the OW would hang out with them. But I trusted in my LORD and let it go.

Another praise is my EH purchased a car for the OW 4-5 months ago. That was painful, and my LORD really worked on me with that and helped me through it. God kept telling me if your enemy is hungry, feed him and if he is thirsty, give him a drink. So, I let it go and gave it to God. Can you believe my husband asked me to help him sell the OW car!? I did just that, I took pictures and placed the ad.

These couple of weeks have been so hard. But I keep seeking Him and trusting Him. I've kept my mouth shut and I have to keep going back to the RYM book and rereading it to keep me in check. I know He is working and when I least expect it He shows me signs. I feel joy and faith in Him! I give You all the glory my Beloved! You are faithful. I honor You, I praise You and I love You. Thank you!

Psalm 86:17 "Show me a sign for good, that those who hate me may see it and be ashamed,

Because You, O Lord, have helped me and comforted me.

Exodus 14:14 "The Lord will fight for you while you keep silent."

Proverbs 3:5-6 "Trust in the Lord with all your heart and do not lean on your own understanding. In all your ways acknowledge Him, and He will make your paths straight."

These Truths are what keep coming in my mind to fight the battle. When I would see so much going on I would say Prov. 3:5 in my mind. Now He is showing me a sign for good.

Chapter 4

Bree

"Your word is a lamp to my feet
and a light to my path."
—Psalm 119:105

"Our Journey Never Ends"

Bree, how did your restoration actually begin?

One week before our 12-year anniversary, my husband left, saying he did not love me anymore. We had been in crisis for about a year and he had been threatening to leave me, but I did not believe he'd really do it. We did not seek help because I thought it was a phase that we were going through. I chalked it up to the financial problems and the stress and routine of everyday life. How wrong I was.

How did God change your situation Bree as you sought Him wholeheartedly?

My life and my situation changed completely the moment I gave my life to the Lord. Then, from that moment, I was no longer alone. He held me in His arms and at every moment I felt nothing other than peace. I'd speak to Him and spent time in His arms. He was more than a Savior or Lord to me. He became my *HH*. When I felt alone or I felt any sort of sadness dominating me, I entered into the secret places of my heart and I'd ask my *HH* to guide me. He began to show me that I needed to become the wise wife He'd designed me to be. Only our *HH* and His love are able to transform us. Entrust your life to Him and He will never once fail you.

What principles, from God's Word (or through our resources), Bree, did the Lord teach you during this trial?

The Bible was my comfort and my guide day-by-day. Just as important was the book *How God Can and Will Restore Your Marriage.* Both were fundamental in my journey. From the moment I applied the principle of letting go, I began to see the difference. The power of forgiveness and how it frees us, to be able to look at our sins and mistakes, no longer the sins of your EH or any other person, is all transforming. Following each principle, renewing my mind in the truth, is when I realized how much I'd failed in my marriage. I finally took the log out of my own eyes. Also, not talking to people about my problems helped me a lot. I stopped making mistakes and doubting what I knew I should do. Speaking to, listening to, and following the Lord by taking His hand, led me on a direct path to peace and my restoration.

What were the most difficult times that God helped you through Bree?

The most difficult times He helped me through were certainly when I found out about the OW. These were the moments when I could not see hope in my future. When my husband claimed that he did not love me, saying that he spent years by my side pretending to love me. Telling me that all those times of sadness, comforting each other, times we'd endured as a couple were not real. But from the moment I began to trust and give everything to my *HH*, asking Him, "Reveal to me the truth", my burden became lighter and I could see that God put me in this situation for one reason alone: to truly find a Husband who loved me. A Husband who was there beside me just waiting for me to see Him, acknowledge Him and embrace Him. God used these very difficult moments, moments when I was shattered, to transform me into a better person.

Bree, what was the "turning point" of your restoration?

The turning point happened the moment I realized it was time to really let go. Never to call him, never to send him a single message for any reason and to ask absolutely nothing from my earthly husband ever. From that moment on, I had a Husband and I knew I must be faithful to Him alone.

Tell us HOW it happened Bree? Did your husband just walk in the front door? Bree, did you suspect or could you tell you were close to being restored?

A few weeks before my husband returned, I went through times of immense trial. People, even members of my own family told me that I should move on, find someone who would be better for me. It seemed as if everyone I knew had to tell me how perfect my EH and the OW were for each other. How happy they always were. And because I was so happy with Who I'd found, my HH, I began to think, "No, I really don't want my marriage restored."

Even with all of this, I felt deep down that our story as a married couple had not ended and that I had to trust my HH for my future. It had already been 16 months since he had left and during that time period there were regular returns, but then he'd leave again. Without having my own Love by my side, never taking my eyes off of Him nor yearning for a man who clearly cared for someone else, I know I would have reacted badly.

The truth is, the reason more marriages aren't restored, is because we want things done now when the delay just means we are not ready yet. More transformation, more healing needs to be done in our lives. This process needs the constant nurturing of Someone who truly loves and cares about us. So rather than want the restoration to occur, we become so content the wait is pleasurable.

My restoration happened after 18 months and 5 days. Without any signs or warnings (other than what I understood as signs when the enemy turns up the heat). One day out of nowhere my husband called me asking if we could talk. When we met, he wept, and he asked me for my forgiveness. He said he was ashamed for everything he put me through. He said that he loved me and always did even when he said he didn't. He said that without me he'd be lost, he'd be without anything that mattered to him. He said he'd understand if I wanted to move on but begged me to consider taking him back.

I stood up, leaned over, whispered "I love you" and we drove home in one car. This happened 4 months and 2 days ago. Though I now see I should have submitted my testimony sooner, I guess I wasn't sure He was done with me, done with us yet. Now I understand our journey never ends with restoration and I am so glad. I never want to stop the relationship I found with Him and I never want to replace what we have with an earthly relationship that leaves me wanting.

Would you recommend any of our resource in particular that helped you Bree?

Yes the book *How God Can and Will Restore Your Marriage* and also the *courses* that allow us to journal and speak and hear from Him. This makes the journey enjoyable and today I love to go back and read those love letters I wrote to Him and He wrote to me. I also suggest to everyone, to every woman *Finding your Abundant Life* and *Living the*

Abundant Life. I am on the fourth abundant life book now and each has helped solidify my marriage.

Would you be interested in helping encourage other women Bree?

Yes

Either way Bree, what kind of encouragement would you like to leave women with, in conclusion?

Trust in the Lord for your salvation, then take His hand, make Him your One and Only. Rest in Him, do not follow the advice of the world, for only He knows what is going on. Follow the principles of the Bible and what's clearly taught here at RMI. Practice patience and forgiveness with everyone. Go beyond just praying and begin to communicate with your HH as a true Husband. Give your life and your problems to Him, give your future to Him.

"Your word is a lamp to my feet and a light to my path" Psalm 119

"I will say of the Lord, He is my refuge and my fortress, and I will trust in him" Psalm 91

Chapter 5

Zelda

"The wise woman builds her house,
but the foolish tears it down
with her own hands."
—Proverbs 14:1

"Almost Everyday I Asked for a Divorce"

Zelda, how did your restoration actually begin?

Well my beloved sisters. I first confess that I was a foolish woman who destroyed and tore her marriage down with her own hands. Two years ago is when I was separated from my husband. My husband started the divorce proceedings because I despised everything. Being married bothered me, so almost every day I asked him for a divorce. I was blind, possessed by selfishness that told me that I did not love my husband. A lie of the enemy. God told me many times through His Word and through many sisters.

So many told me that the Lord says to repent, what you are doing is wrong. Stop before you act! My EH had already committed adultery with another woman, and the worst thing was that I did not care!! And instead, I want a husband who makes me feel special. Then one day I see my husband with that woman and it feels like my heart burst out of my chest. Oh, what terrible anguish I felt when I saw him with her. I drop to my knees and plead with God for help.

Then, the LORD, MY HEAVENLY Husband, and Father show me the first pages of the book GOD WANTS AND CAN RESTORE YOUR MARRIAGE. I decide to read it and decide, yes I want my marriage restored and thought all I have to do is decide I want it and pray in agreement with our group. But everything is a process, it's a journey.

The truth was my EH despised me and even though I wanted everything to happen quickly, I began to understand that the times of GOD are PERFECT AND WE HAVE TO WAIT. I saw changes in me but I did not realize or see that GOD WAS WORKING IN THE LIFE OF MY HUSBAND. I had to learn to release my husband and to stop my obsession of following him at midnight to see if he was with the other woman.

It was almost a full year of not knowing when I RECEIVED A CALL FROM HIM. He told me he wanted to speak with me. When we met he said he had stopped the DIVORCE PROCESS, GOD had him stop it!

My husband returned home and we are finally together. My HUSBAND RETURNED HOME WE ARE TOGETHER. This month we are planning to give each other new rings and renew our marriage vows.

Many thanks to the one who shared the first pages and the book HOW GOD WANTS AND CAN RESTORE YOUR MARRIAGE and also for my group who was praying in agreement.

I want to ENCOURAGE each of you to follow His plan and don't give up because GOD IS FAITHFUL and always MEETS and exceeds His PROMISES.

I LOVE YOU all, IN THE LOVE OF GOD,

Zelda

How did God change your situation Zelda as you sought Him wholeheartedly?

God was wonderful in teaching me so much, mostly that He is faithful and always fulfills His promises. Also that this is a process, a journey but to value each day of this with Him.

What principles, from God's Word (or through our resources), Zelda, did the Lord teach you during this trial?

I learned a lot from the RYM and also from studying the testimonials that I read here.

What were the most difficult times that God helped you through Zelda?

In my despair, I saw everything as lost, but now I know that with God there is nothing impossible!

Zelda, what was the "turning point" of your restoration?

The return of my husband and him telling me that he never stop loving me.

Tell us HOW it happened Zelda? Did your husband just walk in the front door? Zelda, did you suspect or could you tell you were close to being restored?

He called me and said he wanted to talk to me and that's how everything started and how my restoration journey was completed. The Lord taught me to trust in Him with all my heart, not what I saw.

Would you recommend any of our resource in particular that helped you Zelda?

Everything from your ministry was very helpful, for me, it was mainly each of the *By the Word of Their Testimonies* books that I studied.

Would you be interested in helping encourage other women Zelda?

Of course! Yes.

Either way Zelda, what kind of encouragement would you like to leave women with, in conclusion?

May each of you continue moving forward and do not feel defeated even though you see that nothing is happening. God is working with our husbands and when you least expect it, there is your victory!!

Chapter 6

Renata

"With people this is impossible,
but with God all things are possible."
—Matthew 19:26

"Show Me What To Do. Please Lead Me"

Ashlee, how did Renata's restoration actually begin?

This testimony I'm submitting is for a close friend, Renata, a colleague who had been married for many years and has 2 children. We work together. I noticed from one particular comment that she was not well. Upon receiving the news that another coworker had just gotten married, I heard her say, "We all want to marry, but so many find themselves separating..." That's when I realized that something was wrong. I learned from another colleague that she had left home and was in the process of filing a legal separation from her husband. I felt immediately compelled by the Lord to do something. So, I asked Him, "Just show me what to do. Please lead me."

During my lunch hour, I went to a copier and printed the first chapter of the book *How God Can and Will Restore Your Marriage.* I asked the Lord to give me the proper opportunity to talk to her and to give me the right words for our conversation. On that same day, the opportunity came. We talked, and I shared what I was going through. Then she opened up, not giving details, but summed up the problem she was experiencing in her marriage. She said that she loved her husband very much and that there was no other man and she had no intention of looking for another man. There was no other woman in her husband's life either. The fact was that she could no longer live with her husband's aggressive temper. According to her, the husband had a very bad heart beside the fact that he had issues with excessive drinking. She shared that her husband's actions alienated the entire family and on several occasions, he exposed her and humiliated her in public especially when he drank.

Fights and humiliations also happened in the presence of their children. She said that her concept of the world was totally different from that of the husband. Because she had a very difficult life, she has learned to help and to pity her neighbor. Her husband, according to her, is a bitter, spiteful, selfish person, unable to help anyone. Her greatest sorrow was that her husband had not accepted her sick father into their home. The father while very weak, was asked to leave her house after her husband told him to get out and her dad never returned. Just three months later her father passed away. It hurt her deeply.

Although she professed to still loving her husband, she was determined to continue the separation because she no longer believed that there would be a change in her husband and she had come to the conclusion that she wanted to be happy. She had suffered all her married life and did not want to stay in a marriage only to continue suffering. She did not want the children to see any more quarrels and humiliations.

How did God change Renata's situation Ashlee as she sought Him wholeheartedly?

My friend told me, after reading the *RYM* book that she was willing to fight for her marriage and family. I told her to fight, but only with the spiritual weapons He provides. I told her that God can transform any situation. He works miracles. Even though it appears as a full restoration, I believe she's still at the beginning of the restoration process. The fact that she came home and is willing to trust God is only a small step on the journey she's being called to travel. What I want is to continue to be used by Him to help this family and am so thankful that He continues giving me opportunities to help her by passing on everything that God has said to me in my heart.

What principles, from God's Word (or through our resources), Ashlee, did the Lord teach Renata during this trial?

As I talked to her, I was able to share about some principles in the RYM book. First, God told her not to give up on her marriage, that she should not insist or continue trying to change her husband because no one can change the heart of man, only God Himself. And I told her to make a 3x5 card for that verse:

"The king's heart is like channels of water in the hand of the LORD; He turns it wherever He wishes." Proverbs 21:1

I told her to not try to figure out what to do or not do, but instead to simply ask Him what to do or say, which is acknowledging He is right there with her and it's how He will guide her. I told her to add this verse to her cards:

"Trust in the LORD with all your heart and do not lean on your own understanding. In all your ways acknowledge Him, and He will make your paths straight." Proverbs 3:4-6

I told her to have faith in God and to seek a relationship with her Heavenly Husband with all her heart at this moment and forever. I told her only God would bring the peace and joy that she needed to get through this storm. I shared the mistakes I'd made during my journey, mistakes I wanted her to avoid. As I did her eyes filled with tears. I realized that what she had said was true, that it was not a lack of love, but a weariness due to years of struggling in the flesh to transform a situation and her husband. I told her that regardless of her religion (she is Catholic), our God is the God of the impossible, the God who works miracles. Is there anything too hard for God?

Then I opened my Bible to these verses and told her to write them on her cards and underline "with God":

Matthew 19:26—
And looking at them Jesus said to them, "With people this is impossible, but with God all things are possible."

Mark 10:27—
Looking at them, Jesus said, "With people it is impossible, but not with God; for all things are possible with God."

Luke 1:37—
"For nothing will be impossible with God."

Luke 18:27—
But He said, "The things that are impossible with people are possible with God."

Finally, I asked her to again remember, she needs His love, the love of a Husband in order for her to be healed and comforted. That during the times we women need that so much, she needed that relationship with Him. I told her to write down these two verses on another card:

Psalm 37:4—
"Delight yourself in the Lord and He will give you the desires of your heart."

Isaiah 54:4-6—

"Fear not, for you will not be put to shame; and do not feel humiliated, for you will not be disgraced; but you will forget the shame of your youth, and the reproach of your widowhood you will remember no more.

"For your Husband is your Maker, Whose name is the Lord of hosts; And your Redeemer is the Holy One of Israel, Who is called the God of all the earth.

"'For the Lord has called you, Like a wife forsaken and grieved in spirit, Even like a wife of one's youth when she is rejected,' Says your God."

"Instead of your shame you will have a double portion, and instead of humiliation they will shout for joy over their portion. Therefore they will possess a double portion in their land, Everlasting joy will be theirs. For I, the Lord, love justice, I hate robbery...and I will faithfully give them their recompense and make an everlasting covenant with them. Then their offspring will be known among the nations, and their descendants in the midst of the peoples."

I told her to underline or highlight each word that confirms He'd heard and will answer her cries for help.

What were the most difficult times that God helped Renata through Ashlee?

For me personally, it was to let go and trust that she needed a relationship with her *HH* more than with me. I needed to remember that she needed to trust that God would restore her marriage just as I had said and what the book says.

I'm grateful because I learned through the *courses* and *Encourager* each day how important it is to make room in our relationships. I would say we're still not close friends, just co-workers. We speak sporadically, and our interactions are mostly professional and work-related. From the moment I delivered the book to her (I ordered a paperback after giving her chapter 1 and then when she said she wanted to read the full book, after I gave her the full eBook), and I told her to focus on God, I gave her room to read the book and let her look for me when she felt like it. I told her that I would be agreeing with her and trusting God for her family to be fully restored. I told her that I was available whenever she needed it and that she could talk to me anytime.

I was careful not to ask or prompt her for details. And one point she began to open up more, but it was clearly revealing her husband's sins, not hers. So, I stopped her and shared the principle of the curse Genesis 9:22–25. Then I shared the example of Abigail in 1 Samuel 25 and how she'd shamed her husband and how this resulted in her hurting her own children's future. I told her I'd learned this in another book from RMI, *A Wise Woman*, and that if she wanted to go through this book, I would order us both copies, so we could study it together.

Ashlee, what was the "turning point" of Renata's restoration?

Today, almost two months after we talked, she came to me. She said she moved back home to their house two days after reading the RYM book. She said she apologized to her husband for leaving and she said that her change of heart made an impact on how he reacted. This was the first sign that God is working on her behalf. She said they are still in the process of adapting as a couple, different than the way they've ever been before. She said they are talking rather than fighting.

For me, the most exciting thing is that they are reading the books, *A Wise Woman*, and *A Wise Man* together and for the first time he went to church with her and the children. Then she said he found a church closer to their home, a church that is not Catholic, but she says she has already heard the pastor quoting verses she has written on her cards. So she said she knows this is God confirming that her husband is going to change and take his place as their family's spiritual leader.

Tell us HOW it happened Ashlee? Did Renata's husband just walk in the front door? Ashlee, did Renata suspect or could she tell she was close to being restored?

I do not know the specifics of what led her to return home. The fact is that she went back, and I believe I will see the full transformation and restoration of this precious family.

About a week ago, she said that her husband became very ill, but I told her not to pray to God for the cure but rather for God to work His will in her husband's life. I explained the principle that in some situations God allows suffering to produce brokenness in the heart of man. She concurred that she has noticed a change, a meekness in him, a humility that wasn't there before.

Would you or Renata recommend any of our resource in particular that helped you minister Ashlee? Or what you know helped Renata the most?

The book *How God Can and Will Restore Your Marriage* is tremendous. It was the way God used me to hope again and to sow hope in the lives of other women not just in Renata's life. As He led me and RMI suggests doing, I simply give chapter 1 of RYM and if I see the heart is open, then I offer more.

As far as Renata, I've personally seen and heard her recommending A Wise Woman and A Wise Man to coworkers who are married. She's been very discreet, not sharing her own marriage difficulties, which is why I believe she hasn't mentioned the RYM book to anyone.

I would have recommended the online courses, but I knew the only computer she has access to is at work and she doesn't have a phone capable of doing the *courses*. But I do recommend the *courses* to everyone who can do them.

Would you be interested in helping encourage other women Ashlee? Would Renata?

Yes, I hope to continue to be used by Him and I already can see that He is using Renata to help strengthen and encourage women too.

Either way Ashlee, what kind of encouragement would you or Renata like to leave women with, in conclusion?

This marriage is still in the process of restoration, but it is a restoration since she is home, and I can see that as a couple they are together, walking this journey together as He leads. The fact that she returned home, which was such a huge step, but then went on to allow God to begin to change her husband rather than doing it herself. I know that "He who has begun the good work in this family is Who will complete it!" I believe that God will continue to turn the wilderness of our workplace into springs of water so we all become fruitful in our married lives. I am very thankful because somehow, I know that God used me to bring encouragement to this woman and to help prevent a family from destruction. In the past, I would have said nothing and years ago, I would have been the loudest voice telling her that she should leave her husband.

For someone who has such little fruit in my own restoration, seeing this is a cause of great joy for me! Although my own marriage has not yet been restored, the joy of knowing that I am somehow helping someone comforts me and gives me hope and confirms the Lord's faithfulness in all things. God knew that "I would have despaired unless I had believed that I would see the goodness of the Lord in the land of the living. Wait on the Lord, be of good courage, yes, wait on the Lord." Psalm 27:13. Now I know that during my wait He has called me and given me the tools from RMI to help many women find hope and help them set off on the right course along their journey. I can't tell you just how this has changed my life.

Chapter 7

Vinita

"So will My word be which goes forth from My mouth;
It will not return to Me empty, without accomplishing
what I desire, and without succeeding
in the matter for which I sent it."
—Isaiah 55:11

"Spreading the Truth I was Absorbing"

Vinita, how did your restoration actually begin?

The grace and peace of our Lord and Savior and Beloved *HH*!

It all started when my husband was promoted, and we discovered we were not able to build a house in the city where we lived. So, we decided that at the beginning I would stay here and then visit him every three months. My husband is a physicist, very serious and dedicated to research. However, the enemy knows exactly our weak points and took advantage of us foolishly thinking we could live apart. I had already purchased a ticket to visit him at Christmas when I received his phone call saying that I should not come since his heart was cooling towards me and he wanted to rethink our marriage and future together. I was in shock. I almost had a heart attack. I could not believe what I was hearing. There was nothing I could do. I hung up and I cried a lot. I had no idea what I could do, I really could not do anything.

The moment I hung up the phone, I dropped to my knees and cried out with the most sorrowful prayer of my life. I immediately felt the comfort of the Lord, with the understanding that He never abandons us. I cried for a week and did not feel like eating. My flesh was weak, I had chills and became quite ill, but during this time I never ceased to pray and ask God to hold me in that very distressing moment of my life and show me what to do.

How did God change your situation Vinita as you sought Him wholeheartedly?

After the first of the year, I spent the whole night crying. At dawn I took a train (I had been staying at a friend's house) and I went back home. I was totally in communion with God, in prayer and without realizing I'd been fasting for more than four days. The train was almost empty, when suddenly I heard a voice saying to me, "Daughter I am here, do not fear, I am the Alpha and the Omega, the beginning and the end, besides Me there is no other." I was desperate thinking that I was going crazy, I had to be sure that voice was not a production of my imagination, an allusion of some sort due to not eating and being in so much distress. Then I realized I began to be surrounded by an inexplicable peace. I asked to be baptized by the Holy Spirit, and as soon as I finished asking, I began to be filled with the Spirit and I began to speak in tongues right there on the train!

For more than 22 years I've been an evangelical believer, but I'd heard of the power and it had been a secret desire of mine. At that moment, my life changed, I became strong and with great faith. My daughter was very happy for me and my communion with God was absolutely wonderful.

What principles, from God's Word (or through our resources), Vinita, did the Lord teach you during this trial?

Only two days after this encounter, I am sure that it was the Lord who guided me to the RMI website. I read the entire book, then I downloaded the book *How God Can and Will Restore Your Marriage* . I've always loved to read and I thought I knew all His teachings, but this book showed me I had no principles that I lived by. Very soon I was putting each principle into practice: I never called my husband, and I have to say just this one principle, to let go, really helped me a lot.

Each lesson I identified with as if God was speaking directly to me! I asked God's forgiveness for each of my mistakes, in each journal. Despite my being a calm and sweet person, as my friends say, I didn't realize just how argumentative I really have always been. To strengthen my resolve to change, anytime He gave me the opportunity, I talked about each course, each principle I was learning with my daughter and as many friends as possible in order to spread all the truth I was absorbing.

What were the most difficult times that God helped you through Vinita?

A month later, my sister saw a post on facebook (I had deleted mine as the course says is wise) and she told me that my husband was seriously dating another woman. It felt like a sword was piercing my heart. She showed me the photos of them and where he said that he loved her! And soon after, he posted how he'd became engaged.

That's when I sought my Lord the most. His voice told me to fast for 40 days, so I skipped both breakfast and lunch and only ate a very small meal at five in the evening. During these 40 days during my skipped meals, I fell in love with my *HH* so much. I could feel how His love was healing my soul.

I had not been working because my husband had always provided for us. So I had no idea how I was able to pay our rent or buy food, but we did. Then, after eight months, God opened the door for a job for me, and soon after, I was able to buy a car. HE is wonderful! I could never have imagined living like this, supernaturally. As Erin says, as His bride we will live abundantly! Hallelujah!!

After a few more months of studying law, I passed the entrance exam to practice law, but more than anything, people saw the glory of God in my life. He gave me an entire makeover. I had lost close to 60 pounds and I looked younger than when my husband had left. People in my former church saw me (I also let go of my church to become His bride and join RF) but instead of being shunned as I'd feared, people in my church revered me as a wise woman of God. I came to love helping other women who were going through the same thing, just as Erin taught us.

My suffering became only longing, I only loved and longed for my Heavenly Husband. I only thought of Him, how faithful He was, how He was my Friend, my Companion, and how much He cared for me in every detail of my life. Praise the Lord!.

Vinita, what was the "turning point" of your restoration?

One day my former pastor contacted me and said, "I believe that you need to share your testimony at our church. Would you come this Sunday and share what He's done in your life?" I have always been very shy but knew I had to face my fears and honor the Lord. I knew He would speak through me and help me share the testimony of how this crisis was the best thing to happen to me. I wanted everyone to know God is wonderful and can change even the most impossible situation.

It was wonderful to free myself from shyness and fear. That Sunday I spoke in the power of His love sharing with His people, how now, in my heart there was no more sorrow or pain. I had been healed by His Love, by being His bride. The congregation was moved and the result was tremendous. I was asked to head up a women's wise woman course, but asked that it not be held in the church but in a home.

Each month we've doubled in our numbers and have had to open new homes. Now we meet on almost every day during the week. To think how God used this crisis and a person such as I am to do so much as this!

Tell us HOW it happened Vinita? Did your husband just walk in the front door? Vinita, did you suspect or could you tell you were close to being restored?

The day my husband contacted me was sudden. I just did not realize that the Lord would change everything so suddenly and to be honest, I wanted things to remain as they were, just me and Him.

It happened soon after I spoke at my former church, and I made the decision to make Him my only goal. My husband contacted me and said he was going to be in town and could he please sleep on the couch in my house. I sought my *HH* and I invited him to stay. He came, we spoke very little, and I went to bed. When I woke up he had the couch made up but wasn't there.

A few hours later he came back and we had lunch together. After lunch, I went to our room. Then I heard a knock at the door asking if he could please talk to me.

He told me that he'd ended his relationship with the other woman, that he had bought a new house in another nearby town. Then he stopped, he just looked at me and then finally asked if I wanted to come and live with him and "restore" our marriage. He used the word "restore."

I told him that whatever God was calling me to do, I would do. And I said I believed God wanted us to rebuild our family on the Rock. He said that he understood from God that it was the right thing to do, that it would be a new beginning for us.

The next thing he did was to stand up and take something out of His pocket, he put his wedding ring back on his finger, which he said he had taken off the day he left the house and took the job in the other city. He said he was ashamed because he told himself he was a single man even though he wasn't.

I asked him about us remarrying again, but he looked puzzled. Then he said he had canceled the divorce, but I had never been notified.

In all, it was almost 29 months of separation.

Today it's been almost 6 months since we moved into our new house, in a new city, to live our new life as a wise couple. The Wise Woman classes still go on, but without me.

At one point he wanted to talk to me and share everything that he did while we were apart, but I interrupted him and said it didn't matter. It was God who started the Good Work of Faith and it's what He used to change us both. He says he loves me more than ever and I say the same thing because of the love I have from my HH.

Would you recommend any of our resource in particular that helped you Vinita?

I highly recommend the book *How God Can and Will Restore Your Marriage* and to read the *Daily Encourager* every single day. Every woman who I meet, I suggest they take the *online courses* to prevent what happened to me. I tell them to journal and to submit frequent praise reports in order to continue building each other up.

We must turn our full attention to our *HH* so that our hearts are fully His. The healing you need will only happen through the love of the perfect Husband. And once healed, it's important that we become a vessel to be used to build up other women. No matter how shy or how much you feel you can't be used. Just believe! And tell Him you are His to use.

Would you be interested in helping encourage other women Vinita?

YES! We must all be vessels.

Either way Vinita, what kind of encouragement would you like to leave women with, in conclusion?

I want to leave this for each of my sisters who are in the desert. My encouragement of faith is this: Do not give up, for on your side is the One who owns the universe, for this God that you and I serve, NOTHING IS IMPOSSIBLE for Him. You just need to let go of this world and if you would simply put Him as your first and only Love, everything beautiful will happen to you. May the Lord be your peace always and forever.

Chapter 8

Ariana

"I came that they may have life,
and have it abundantly."
—John 10:10

"He Wants Us to Have it All"

Ariana, how did your restoration actually begin?

My husband began acting very strange, but every time I confronted him
he said that it was just the stress at work. Then one day he just
disappeared, vanished. When he returned a week later, he said that he
had gone to clear his head. Just a month later, he disappeared for 10
days. This time when he reappeared, he confessed that he had an OW.
He said it had been going on for almost a year. He'd met her on the
internet and he said he was looking because of all the fights our entire
marriage. As the fights intensified, he said he decided to meet her
personally, although she lived in another state. He said when they met
"she liked me, and I liked her a lot too."

After this confession, nothing more was said. We just coexisted
together for about a month. During this month I confronted him all the
time for more details, I rummaged through his things, and this resulted
in many fights. One day I discovered my husband had left his phone
unlocked and I found the OW texts. I exchanged messages with her,
and she said that she did not know that he was married. He confirmed
that this fact was true, she didn't know. That very day he packed
everything and left home. Before he left, he handed me his wedding
ring and said that it was all over between us.

**How did God change your situation Ariana as you sought Him
wholeheartedly?**

The day after he left, I found the RMI ministry on the internet and read
the book, *How God Can and Will Restore Your Marriage*. I read it
cover to cover without stopping. The next day I read it again, and then

again. As I began to apply the principles over the next two months, day after day my husband's heart began to turn back towards me. The rejection was not easy. During the first few times we interacted again, he said he was sure he wanted to actually end our marriage. Yet I knew that God was in control.

When he left I didn't know where he was, then I discovered he went to live with his parents. I believe it was only because the OW lived in another state. While my husband was in contact with me, they met together alone from time to time, and when the topic came up, he assured me that he was determined to stay with her. Yet the Lord was changing me, He was changing my life, and little by little I watched as God turned my husband's heart back to me.

What principles, from God's Word (or through our resources), Ariana, did the Lord teach you during this trial?

The principle of letting go and the principle of winning without words were the fundamental principles I learned that made the greatest change. These were also the most difficult, since I am part of a generation who have been taught to be talkative, possessive, and horribly contentious women. Each time I counted it a miracle to be close to him without me speaking and becoming controlling. As the months past, he began to approach me very slowly, he'd drive by or come to my house. He began to call me and ask me out. Each time I would keep quiet and I would only answer, gently, if he asked me!

What were the most difficult times that God helped you through Ariana?

The worst times were when he first traveled to the other state to see the OW. He'd just disappear. He'd leave without his family knowing where he'd gone and disappear for different lengths of time without any news. When he left he would turn off his cell phone and vanish. During these times I prayed, fasted and sought God. Then, just as suddenly he'd send a message. Sometimes he contacted me only asking for his daughter, but I gave glory to God because He gave me a sign of life. I was worried about him on the road.

Ariana, what was the "turning point" of your restoration?

Without a doubt, the turning point was to first let go but then to seek the face of God. It was then I'd finished the first 3 *courses* and wanted more. Then I heard about the *Abundant Life* series. That's when I was first introduced and fell in love with my Heavenly Husband. At that moment I was finally able to rest, knowing that only God could bring him back, not me. My part was only to trust my *HH* and rest in the God of the impossible to restore my marriage.

I began to literally feast on the Bible, AND I read it through using the *Bible* program suggested. Living my life abundantly wasn't something I ever knew was possible, certainly not when my life had been deep in the valley of despair, in the heat of the dry desolate desert. Yet this is when my life turned around and soon after, so did my marriage.

Tell us HOW it happened Ariana? Did your husband just walk in the front door? Ariana, did you suspect or could you tell you were close to being restored?

I honestly did not imagine it could happen so fast. It happened just two months after really embracing my Husband, letting go of restoration, and settling into a life I had never dreamed was possible.

It happened on a Saturday when he asked if he could come by to talk. He sat down and simply said that we had to get it right, that he wanted to rebuild our marriage. He said he was no longer involved with the OW. He said he'd told her it was wrong, that I was different. He wanted to end everything and please never contact him again. He said that he'd told his parents and packed up all of his belongings that were in the car. He asked if I was willing to give us another try (because I'd kept silent the entire time he spoke), and I nodded yes.

Would you recommend any of our resource in particular that helped you Ariana?

First, reading How God Can and Will Restore Your Marriage as many times as you can to renew your mind and rid yourself of the lies. Then get your home ready for your husband's return by reading *A Wise Woman*. Both of these I'd suggest the *online courses* in order to journal, to confess, and to go back often to see your progress. It's what really kept me going.

The real change in your life will happen when you discover your *HH*. I finally understood how this was possible by doing the abundant life series beginning with *Finding the Abundant Life Course*.

Would you be interested in helping encourage other women Ariana?

Yes of course!

Either way Ariana, what kind of encouragement would you like to leave women with, in conclusion?

Do not give up on your marriage, especially when everything seems impossible. It's true that God turns the heart of the husband back to their wives. Yet this doesn't fully happen until our hearts are completely His.

Your husband has no free will! God is in control! God is faithful and He who believes in the Lord will never be disappointed! Never! Hallelujah! Only God can restore a marriage! You can't do it and those who try, find themselves worn out and discouraged. Your *HH* is waiting for you and once you're His— GOD will restore your marriage just as He did with me. I did not deserve to have a new life, to live abundantly, but God is faithful! Glory to God forever! He wants us to have it all.

Chapter 9

Shay

"Delight yourself in the Lord; and
He will give you the desires of your heart"
—Psalm 37:4

"Our Lives Became Calm"

Shay, how did your restoration actually begin?

It all started when we had been married a little more than four years. But I guess it was only after we'd been married for six months that I began to notice changes in my husband. I did not pay attention, I tried to ignore it, but that's when we began to fight a lot and it's when I first started to distrust my husband.

It took four years to find what had gone wrong. I went to look at some things of his and discovered he'd had an OW in his life all the time we were married. Devastated, I confronted him, but he denied everything. Without proof, I couldn't do anything, not until the moment that I discovered him looking at love messages on his cell. I stood behind him watching them exchange love notes. That moment was the death of me!

When he spun around, and our eyes met, he knew he couldn't lie anymore. He cried, asked me for forgiveness and said, "I promise, I'll end it." Yet over time I discovered that they were still very much together. This lasted for close to a year and a half. I would write long letters to God and in each, I begged Him to end this situation my husband was in. I told God I could not take any more. I couldn't go on like this any longer. I wanted her gone.

But rather than wait for God, one day I picked up his phone, found her phone number and called to confront her. My husband was furious with me, but she then said that she was with him because she did not know that he was married. That was a lie, in fact, I know she knew. But I really wanted him to leave me, because I really began to loathe him.

So, at that moment I basically tore my house down what little was still standing.

How did God change your situation Shay as you sought Him wholeheartedly?

After that incident, when I was clearly no longer interested in my husband, apparently, they separated and stopped their relationship. At first my husband was just a little better with me, but not much. I continued to distrust him. I had no reason to believe him and I quite honestly feared caring at all, not wanting to through everything again.

A year went by, and he was soon unemployed, and we became much closer. I gave him my full support and did so with joy believing our troubles were behind us. After a month, he got a job that would turn out to be temporary. This job took him away from home, he would stay a whole week in another state, and would only come home at the end of the week. I missed him a lot, but during our time apart he came back and was very loving towards me. He'd say that he loved me always, how good that I did not give up on him, that he wanted to grow old with me, and that he had never been so happy.

When it came near his time to leave this job, I prayed a lot and asked God to find someone who was willing to employ him. Give him a good job for us, and for the sake of our marriage. I asked for a job that would not disrupt our lives. And so, God heard and answered. He got a job that was far different than anything he'd done before, and something he liked very much. We were so happy that we scheduled a second honeymoon. We took the trip "of our dreams" but from the beginning, something told me that something was about to happen. Something drastic was up ahead. And that's what happened. A month after our trip, my husband went back to being like before.

What principles, from God's Word (or through our resources), Shay, did the Lord teach you during this trial?

I realized that I'd been begging God to change my situation, to get rid of the OW, to change my husband. But I never asked Him why this was happening. What was His plan for my life? The moment I did I discovered RMI. A friend handed me the *How God Will Restore Your Marriage* book and that's when I saw myself and understood why this was repeating over and over and what needed to be done to change it.

When I got my evaluation back after filling out the questionnaire, right then I saw it. The verse where He said I'd left my first love. I'd left Him long ago and that for women like me, forsaken and grieved, I'd been looking at a man to make it right. What I needed and Who I needed was a Heavenly Husband, a warrior, who would do battle in the heavens to stop the madness I was living through.

What were the most difficult times that God helped you through Shay?

The most difficult was when I found out, that in fact, when I "thought" he'd ended the relationship with the OW, he had not. The next was after our second honeymoon trip ended. When I could not believe that I would go through all this again. But this is what led me to wanting to understand why God was letting this happen. What horrible thing had I done to deserve all this? This is when I started looking on the internet for help, when I found the RMI ministry, when I read the book *How God Can and Will Restore Your Marriage* in two days. It's when I read all the other testimonials, and I knew that I was not alone in this battle. I instantly began to have a peace that surpassed all understanding.

It was when I realized that my longing for my husband to be faithful was foolish because I had not been faithful to my Husband. I guess that's when I really knew what it was that was missing from my life and what God had wanted to show me for years.

For the first time in my life, I started praying for His will to be done. I started fasting and letting my flesh, my controlling self, die. During one of my longer fasts, I finally asked God to restore my marriage. I was done trying to fix things myself. I told Him that after finding my real Husband, my true Husband, I knew I'd been unfaithful, which was worse than what my husband had done to me.

About a day later, while I was alone, I began praising God, thanking Him for all the trials and crises and pain I'd gone through, and then I heard a very quiet voice that said, "My daughter your marriage has already been restored, rest now, I am taking care of everything."

The next thing that happened was that the past came rushing into my head, each thing He'd brought me through. I finally began to understand that, in fact, God, had taken me on this journey, using so much to get my attention. Then finally I understood and I cried tears of thankfulness. God never abandoned me, He was with me throughout everything, but my focus had been on my marriage, on changing my husband. I ignored the times when my *HH* was there, wanting me, longing for me. Each time my husband was unfaithful, I was more unfaithful and it wasn't until I took him off the pedestal and turned my eyes towards Him (my HH) that everything changed.

Shay, what was the "turning point" of your restoration?

Without a doubt, the change happened when I read the verse in Isaiah 54:4-6, "Fear not, for you will not be put to shame; And do not feel humiliated, for you will not be disgraced; but you will forget the shame of your youth, and the reproach of your widowhood you will remember no more. For your Husband is your Maker, Whose name is the Lord of hosts; And your Redeemer is the Holy One of Israel, Who is called the God of all the earth. For the Lord has called you, Like a wife forsaken and grieved in spirit, Even like a wife of one's youth when she is rejected,' Says your God."

Lord, I do not know what my life would be like without Your love. I pray for every woman reading this that she will also find you as her Husband. I do not know how to live far from Your presence, which is more important than everything. I know that you want this for every woman.

Tell us HOW it happened Shay? Did your husband just walk in the front door? Shay, did you suspect or could you tell you were close to being restored?

Friends, never give up, believe me, God is protecting you, and is waiting until your heart and focus are where it needs to be. On Him. You've been rejected, you've been humiliated, you've been disgraced. Do you want to forget the shame?

Take the Lord as your Husband, and let God restore your marriage. How often has the Lord called you? Like a wife forsaken and grieved in spirit, even like a wife of one's youth when she is rejected,' Says your God."

Once my heart was completely His, once I "delighted myself in Him" that's when my husband completely changed. It's been nearly nine months since our lives became calm. When the winds stopped blowing in the storm I'd lived all my married life. I am not the same, my husband is not the same and we are not the same as a couple.

Would you recommend any of our resource in particular that helped you Shay?

Yes, I recommend going to *HopeAtLast.com* and filling out the questionnaire. Then take the free *online courses* that are offered. I also encourage women in crisis to buy the paperback of *How God Can and Will Restore Your Marriage* and *A Wise Woman* in order to highlight it and make notes in the margins.

Most importantly is not to wait to acknowledge you've ignored and cheated on your *HH* because it will prolong your restoration; my life is truth of this.

Would you be interested in helping encourage other women Shay?

Yes

Either way Shay, what kind of encouragement would you like to leave women with, in conclusion?

It's as simple as this, "Delight yourself in the Lord, and He will give you the desires of your heart." Trust that GOD will restore, you can't do it. I hope and pray that everyone who is reading my testimony will become His bride, because only then can you be truly and wonderfully happy.

Chapter 10

Violeta

"But let it be the hidden person of the heart,
with the imperishable quality of a gentle and quiet spirit,
which is precious in the sight of God."
—1 Peter 3:4

"I Took Off My Wedding Ring; It Bothered Him the Most"

Violeta, how did your restoration actually begin?

I have to glorify God for what He did for my family. I often read the testimonies and thought that I would never write mine. But nothing is impossible with God.

It all started quickly, soon after we married. We were an example of Christians inside the church, he was an elder and I was the leader of the women's group. We were highly looked up to, and most referred to us as the "perfect couple." The enemy knew this, so he used his clever schemes. We should never have been ignorant of his schemes since we'd been part of the church our entire lives, yet he used schemes to destroy us and to end everything that God had created.

How did God change your situation Violeta as you sought Him wholeheartedly?

I sought the Lord relentlessly with all my heart, begging God to take away the pain that was in my chest because my husband had left me. I prayed to the Lord, I fasted, I sought Him from dawn until dusk. From the beginning, I heard God telling me that He was going to restore my marriage. He told me to wait, simply to wait on Him because He was working in silence.

What principles, from God's Word (or through our resources), Violeta, did the Lord teach you during this trial?

The principle that was hardest for me was to LET GO. When he left I would call him all the time. Wherever he went, I knew I would find him. I pursued him just as I'd told other women to do. As a vigilant stander, I would write, call, and find a way to get there, wherever he was. I knew that it bothered him, that I was actually driving him away. I never realized the damage I was doing until I read the book *How God Can and Will Restore Your Marriage*, that as a stander, I was just standing in the way of my own restoration.

When I read the truth, about letting go, and stopped pursuing, he really began to think I didn't care about him. The very first time he initiated any contact with me was when he called and asked why I did not care about him anymore and why I did not show up where he was. I told him I'd let go and he was free to be happy. Then, I took off my wedding ring and I know that this example of fully letting go bothered him the most.

When I found my Heavenly Husband and fell deeply in love with my first Love, that's when I was able to fully let go. He said later (after our restoration) that he could actually feel in his heart that I was gone. And that's when my husband began to take all the steps to restore our marriage and win me back.

What were the most difficult times that God helped you through Violeta?

The weekends were always painful for me, especially when Sunday service was over, and I had to go home alone. I cried all the way and when I got home I had no tears to cry anymore. Yet the Lord was there comforting me and calming me in the moments of my despair. Then one day God told me to get my Bible, and when I opened my Bible I heard the Lord, my *HH*, speak to me.

He brought me to all the verses that clearly said that our husbands were to be our spiritual leaders, that women were to remain quiet in church, and so many other things I'd learned at the end of *courses 2*, but I dismissed thinking they didn't pertain to me.

He spoke to me about wanting to give me a makeover, to make me new on the inside to match what He'd done on the outside (I had lost close to 50 lbs.). But to do this I needed to leave the church.

After I left, several women from the church contacted me and I was able to share with each one of them the truth I'd believed I was too good for. One woman asked if we could meet so she could hear more, and that is how my new women's group started.

Violeta, what was the "turning point" of your restoration?

When I was seeking the Lord, my *HH*. I wanted to be with Him at all times, at every moment of my waking day, and my focus was no longer my husband, or my marriage being restored. I was focusing on helping other women. So many heard about our group and I began a second group in another city about this time.

I wasn't sure I wanted my marriage restored, but I remember reading in one of the courses that when we were spiritually mature we wanted His will, not our own. So, I told God, "Your will be done."

As I went about town, I ran into many people and each was astonished by my change. Yes, my outward appearance was first, but when they spoke to me each mentioned how "different" I was. I knew they meant my "gentle and quiet spirit" because before I was very forceful and a know-it-all, having the last and final word. The more I wanted and yearned for more of HIM the more He began to transform me.

One day I ran into my husband who said he'd heard from everyone how much I'd changed but he had no idea I'd changed as much as I had. I thanked him, smiled and turned to leave. But as I exited the mall, I could see he was still there, standing and watching me leave.

Tell us HOW it happened Violeta? Did your husband just walk in the front door? Violeta, did you suspect or could you tell you were close to being restored?

As I said, I was no longer looking for my husband or calling him. When we ran into each other, which began happening more and more, I'd make the conversation brief and leave. Then without warning, he sent a message to me: We Need to Talk! His text almost sounded angry but I agreed and met with him.

He told me that he had gone to church and there, God used a sister who had asked how I was. That's when he heard I'd left the church and he'd become alarmed. He was sure I was involved with someone else and came to ask me to stop, saying it was all his fault.

While speaking to my Beloved in my head and heart (the whole time my husband was speaking), I heard Him say to share what really happened, who I was in love with. So, I was able to share everything with him. It felt like I spoke for 5-10 minutes but when I saw my husband crying, I looked out to see it was dark and I knew I'd been talking for hours. I am not sure all I said, but I know I began confessing my faults and at some point, how I'd fallen in love with my first Love, who I'd left soon after we'd met when I got saved.

What I said came from Him, because in the end, while crying, my husband asked if I would be willing to restore our marriage. I said of course, that this would glorify God, and that day we were reunited and intimate as husband and wife.

Would you recommend any of our resource in particular that helped you Violeta?

I recommend the book: *How God Can and Will Restore Your Marriage* and also recommend buying and reading the *devotional* Streams in the Desert. I'd also recommend going through your *online courses* that will eventually lead to finding your *HH*.

Finding the Abundant Life Course is when things really begin to change for me. And if you don't start a group of your own, the easiest way to begin helping other women (and men too) is to have them open their phones and type in *HopeAtLast.com* so they can begin finding hope and the truth.

Would you be interested in helping encourage other women Violeta?

Yes

Either way Violeta, what kind of encouragement would you like to leave women with, in conclusion?

I would like to tell women who are in the desert that God will help you through this difficult time, but know that unless you're really His, and you act like a bride in love, your difficulties will continue. Without becoming His light in this dark world, no one, not even your husband will find his way back. There is truly nothing impossible for God. No matter what your husband is saying, no matter what other people or ministries tell you to do, do not listen to them. The only way to emerge victorious from this battle and experience the impossible, is to put Him first. I am here, today, with the message from God saying, "I am faithful. My Word is truth. Delight yourself in the Lord and I will give you the desires of your heart, every promise and even more."

Chapter 11

Ghita

"The Lord will fight for you
while you keep silent."
—Exodus 14:14

"The Other Woman said She Was Pregnant"

Ghita, how did your restoration actually begin?

My husband went to visit his son and didn't come home. After about a week, he told me he wasn't happy and wanted a divorce. That was April, four years ago. I found out there was an OW and that my husband was living with her. He came home telling me he broke it off with the OW, but was only home for a few weeks before he went back to her. There were about 2 months when my husband just "disappeared." During those two months, I didn't have any contact with him. I was going to church and just wanted my marriage restored. I knew God can do anything because He is in the miracle business.

Then I did an internet search for saving my marriage and came across the RMI website. I felt the Holy Spirit come over me and I knew God led me to RMI. My husband came home in August, once before I found RMI. After he was home that first month, however, he left again, I just wanted to die. I was having health issues with my gallbladder and I was supposed to schedule surgery. Then, in July, my husband was hospitalized for heart trouble. The OW was there at the hospital. I actually spent 2 nights in a hospital room with my husband and the OW. Only by God's grace was He able to help me through that. I was dying inside seeing the OW sitting on the bed with my husband while I sat on the couch.

How did God change your situation Ghita as you sought Him wholeheartedly?

My husband started coming home to see me. The first few times he did, I wasn't home because I was at church or Bible study. My husband was calling to ask me for some paperwork he needed. My husband started showing me affection and telling me he loved me. We became intimate again. The OW became bitter as wormwood. She and my husband were fighting all the time. She was back in contact with her husband and seeing her husband without my husband knowing. The sick feeling in the pit of my stomach was gone. I had inner peace. My husband would drop the OW at work than spend time with me before he picked her up.

What principles, from God's Word (or through our resources), Ghita, did the Lord teach you during this trial?

I was the contentious woman. I was selfish and mean. I treated my husband like a child. I was disrespectful. But I learned to shut my mouth and have a kind and gentle spirit. I learned my husband wasn't the enemy, but a slave of the enemy. I learned my husband is my authority and spiritual leader. It was my own fault that I went through hell on earth separated from my husband. It happened because I stopped putting God first in my life.

What were the most difficult times that God helped you through Ghita?

Having surgery because I was alone. No one was there for me. A friend picked me up from the hospital and took me home.

Also difficult was being at the hospital with my husband and the OW. The OW was sleeping on the bed next to my husband while I slept on the couch. God totally got me through that. He gave peace to be there for my husband and deal with the medical tests and doctors.

Another difficulty was when the OW announced she was pregnant and we didn't know who the father was. She left my husband in October to be with her husband, but then went back to my husband after she found out about the pregnancy. My husband was home with me in October before going back to OW in November.

Ghita, what was the "turning point" of your restoration?

I had my gallbladder removed a couple days before Thanksgiving. I spent the holidays with a friend because I couldn't walk up two flights of stairs to get into my house. When I got home, I had chest pains and ended up back in the hospital. I had another surgical procedure done for heart tests. My husband walked in my hospital room not long after my second surgery and He handed me divorce papers. All I could whisper was "I love you" to him. He told me to read the papers and I did. So much of what the papers said was incorrect. But the basic personal contact information was wrong. I handed them back to him without saying a word and he left. OW texted me later that day how she and my husband were going to get married. I ignored the text and didn't reply. The text came from my husband's phone, but I know it was from OW.

Tell us HOW it happened Ghita? Did your husband just walk in the front door?

Two weeks later, I fasted for 3 days. Flat on my face on my bedroom floor and I cried out to God to take the pain away. I was so used to my husband not being home that I didn't care if he did come home. I can't remember if it was on the last day of my fast or the day after that, but my husband called me and asked me to meet him to talk. When I met my husband, he came up to the van and said he messed up and that he wanted to come home. He was crying and apologized. I found out later the OW left him days before. Her husband had come and picked her up.

Ghita, did you suspect or could you tell you were close to being restored?

I didn't think I was close to restoration. Things kept getting worse. My car broke down, I had surgery, then my husband brought me divorce papers just minutes after I got out of surgery. Yet, I kept my faith that I was close because Erin said when things appear to be getting worse, you're blessing is close. The closer you get to your blessing, the harder the enemy tries to take it from you.

Would you recommend any of our resource in particular that helped you Ghita?

The *RYM* book, *A Wise Woman*, and the *Be Encouraged eVideos*. Read *Psalms and Proverbs* every day. By studying the *By the Word of Their Testimonies* it encouraged me. So did the *Question and Answers* and *Facing Divorce*. I also keep 3x5 cards in my purse and read them constantly.

Do you have favorite Bible verses Ghita? Any that you would like to pass on to women reading your Testimonies? Promises that He gave you?

Romans 4:17 "As it is written, 'A father of many nations have I made you' in the presence of Him whom he believed, even God, who gives life to the dead and calls into being that which does not exist. The Lord is fighting for him (you), he needs only to be still."

Psalm 97:3 "Fire goes before him and consumes his foes on every side."

Exodus 14:14 "The Lord will fight for you; you need only to be still."

Would you be interested in helping encourage other women Ghita?

Of course

Either way Ghita, what kind of encouragement would you like to leave women with, in conclusion?

Never give up! If your journey gets too hard, take it one day at a time. If that's too overwhelming, take it one hour at a time or one minute at a time. Keep praying and resting in Him. I spoke scripture out loud until the panicky feeling left me. Pray a hedge around your marriage and just trust God to do it. God takes everything and makes something good come out of it.

Stay close to the Lord and He will put the pieces of your broken heart and life back together. If I can sit in a car for 2 hours next to the OW while traveling to the hospital then staying in the same room with her for 2 days, anyone can get through their journey. I'm not a strong person. I cried a lot.

Thank You Lord that my husband is living at home. Thank You that we don't fight anymore. I see small changes, and praise you for each. Thank You for being faithful. Thank You that my husband is starting to spend time with our daughter.

Chapter 12

Miranda

"Instead of your shame you will have
a double portion, and instead of humiliation
they will shout for joy over their portion."
—Isaiah 61:7

"WIN Without Words"

Miranda, how did your restoration actually begin?

First, I want to ask your Lord's forgiveness for not writing the testimony of my Restored Marriage each time I knew I should.

It all started in February after we had been married for 12 years. We had just come back from a honeymoon trip and we were planning to have another child.

I always used my husband's cell phone and then one day I saw a message from an OW, I went to talk to him, but he denied everything. I began to investigate, and every day I discovered other things. So, I decided I would just call and confront the OW. She confessed that she was involved with him and I responded by cursing her out and then arguing with her.

When my husband came in, I confront him and told him about the call I'd made. He confessed that he was involved with OW. I fought with him horribly and then told him he could not do this to me. He cried, saying he was very sorry. But then I started to pressure him, saying, if he loved me he would not do this to me. He didn't say anything, but when I stopped ranting and shouting, he said, "But I don't love you anymore." When I heard that, my world fell apart! All I wanted to do was to die. My life began to consist of just crying. I even stopped going to work and I stopped taking care of my son.

That day I began to pray and decided to tell my mother everything. Then I asked her to help me through prayer.

As each day passed, my will to live was diminishing and I could not eat. Everyone was concerned because I was losing weight fast. My mother-in-law kept telling me that I was losing a lot of weight and I always invented an excuse because I did not want to tell anyone what was going on. I did not accept the adultery and hoped that everything would be resolved before anyone found out.

At the request of my husband, I went to see a psychologist and she referred me to a psychiatrist because she said that I was not well and needed treatment.

I could not stop talking about everything with my husband and because of everything, our life was turned upside down. At one point he told me that he had better leave the house, but I begged him not to, so he stayed but was always threatening to leave. Each time I would shout that he could not abandon me and our son, "for what God united man cannot separate." But instead of helping, this only pushed him farther from me emotionally.

It was already May, four months from when my nightmare began, and I just could not stand to suffer anymore but I did not know what else to do. Each time I prayed it seemed things just got worse. So that's when I started searching the Internet for something from God to help me and when I found the RMI I knew it had all been orchestrated by God to save me!

I immediately started to read the testimonies and found out how to order the book "How God Can and Will Restore Your Marriage." When I began to read the book, I could not believe what I was reading. I saw the kind of contentious woman I was, and that the problem was not with my husband but with me. The more I read, the more I convinced myself that I had destroyed my marriage. I had placed my husband in first place in my life and had abandoned the Lord. I realized that He must be the 1st in our life and because He wasn't the center, God turned my husband's heart far from me.

In less than a week I had read the entire book and throughout this same period, all I could do was cry. I cried not due to my husband leaving or saying he didn't love me but crying because I could finally see how foolish and disobedient I was to the Lord. How I had torn my own house down.

So, after reading the book, I set off on my Restoration Journey, waking up and doing the courses beginning with reading the daily encouragement. To tell you the truth, I do not know whether I'd be alive today if I hadn't started on this new path. If the Lord had not sent me to RMI, and I started to learn every day (in the daily encouragements and lessons straight from the Word of God and these being spoken directly into my heart) I know I would have taken my life.

First, I asked the Lord for forgiveness for all my sins and for abandoning Him. Then I asked my husband to forgive me for the contentious, quarrelsome, bossy, argumentative woman I'd been. I told him I'd done this to him because of not knowing what the Bible said about marriage and due to this, I had destroyed his love for me and our marriage.

I knelt at the Lord's feet and began to pray and fast, asking Him to make me a gentle, quiet woman. A woman who wins without a word, to mold me into His likeness, and do His will in my life. I begged Him not to let my home be destroyed. I asked Him to do a makeover on me and give me a new heart.

Sometimes I would fall and talk more than I should have. I would also cry and sometimes I thought I could not take it because I knew that my husband was with me then go to be with the OW. But the Lord never abandoned me and always got me up and made me move on again along my journey.

One day at a church (before I let it go), at the end of the service, the pastor told me that the Lord had shown him that I was going through a very big battle in my life and was not supposed to give up because at the end of that big battle there would be a victory.

Time passed and one day my husband said he was going to have to work two days in a row and that he would not be able to spend my birthday with me.

The next day I called my husband and to my surprise, he didn't answer. It was the OW who answered!! I was back at work, but this sent me into a deep desperation. I got up from my desk and just left to spend time in my car. I wanted to go back in, but I couldn't stop crying. I called him back, told him what had happened, and instead of being understanding, he just said he was not going through this with me anymore.

When we got home I told him he had to choose either me or the OW and to figure it out. I knew I'd messed up, giving him an ultimatum, so

I quietly begged my HH to bless me double for my foolishness. Thankfully he didn't give me an answer (which I know would have been her not me). What he said was that he was going to go stay at his mother's house. He took his suitcase and put it on the floor, so he could sort things out and while he packed, I was able to embrace the gentle and quiet spirit and apply the principles I should have. I told him that no matter how much I loved him and did not want to be separated, I would no longer stand in his way, that he needed to live his life. That day, I let go.

Oh, how it hurt, but I could not resist what I knew I had to do. Let go. He said that he would go to his mother's house and I wondered what she would say. Later he told me that his mother knew everything from the beginning. He said she could not accept what he was doing to me "Glory to God," and I was thankful I'd never told her anything. When he left, he came right back from his mother's house and said that he was going to sleep at home that night but that he would go back to stay there on Saturday.

Saturday came, and he took our son to play ball and continued staying at home without packing his suitcase. Again, he slept at home Saturday to Sunday. On Sunday morning he sat on our bed and said he wanted to talk to me and that he was going to tell me the truth for the first time. He asked if I would give him a period of one month for him to sort out what was going on and not tell anything to his mother. That he thought he loved OW, only to discover that he did not like her that much, not enough to leave his home and family. He said that he liked our home, our life. Of course, I nodded and agreed.

Each day that passed I gave more and more of my life into the hands of God. Each morning he went to work and in order to get there, he drove with the OW. That's because he was a driver for the carpool and the OW was in his van. But then I heard that the next month, July, would be her last month in his van. I heard she had been transferred to work at another location! Look how God works sisters!! He is more powerful and wonderful than our problems when we just let go and give everything into the hands of the Lord.

As soon as I discovered that the book *A Wise Woman* was available in paperback not just online, I bought it immediately. And as I began to read it, I learned so many wonderful things that RYM hadn't shown me. Oh, how could I imagine that I had to be submissive to my husband! This was something I had never done and so many other things that I had never known was God's will for my life. I'd never considered being able to stay at home just to take care of our family. I have always worked outside and divided the bills with my husband. I knew there was nothing I needed to do to make this happen. I simply believed that the Lord would make this impossibility happen. He would incline the heart of my husband to want this.

Throughout my journey, I have been learning to trust and believe that with God nothing is impossible, and He did not want my marriage to end, "for what God united man does not separate." This needed to be sown in my heart, not to blurt out and use to make my husband stay. As I did, I knew He would make every change needed to make our marriage and home life the way He wanted it to be.

I also stopped going to church because I was going alone and wanted a spiritual leader. I continued praying and fasting for God to continue working in my life and to put me in the place that He wants, and that only He can incline the heart of my husband to do His will, to put back all his desire to serve God again.

More important than anything was that our family be spiritually restored, and my husband become our spiritual leader. One day my husband told me that my prayers were working (I never said I was praying), but he said something was changing in his mind and heart. He said, "God is wonderful, isn't He?" Soon after he began to be affectionate with me, attentive and paying more attention to our son. Out of nowhere, he said that he was hoping I still wanted another child and he also said that I am different and that he loves me very much.

He said that he would not leave home anymore and that he will never abandon us. That's when he said that he and the OW were no longer together, although she still sometimes called him. But he told me not to worry, because he would always hang up. I am praying that the OW will lose interest in my husband and her heart will turn back to her own husband. I believe that the One who started the good work will do all this in His appointed time, for He is the God of the impossible.

I ask each of you who are reading my testimony to never give up giving your problems to God because when the fight feels heavy it means you are trying to do it. When you let go, that's when God comes in and changes everything and rewrites the story. Just as He changed mine, He will change yours as well. Just trust Him. Honestly, I don't have enough words to thank my Lord for all that He has done and for all that He continues to do in our family. Thank you, Erin, for your dedication to helping us through by using only the Word of God and testimonies as proof. May the Lord continue to bless you, your family and this Ministry that speaks directly to our hearts. LORD, I LOVE YOU!!!

How did God change your situation Miranda as you sought Him wholeheartedly?

The Lord called me, and I heard Him through the pain. A pain that seemed to want to kill and it was from there that He began to show me the way forward for my transformation.

Through prayer and fasting and obedience to the Lord, He began to make my transformation. We cannot do anything ourselves except through the spirit of the Lord to change us and transform our hearts.

What principles, from God's Word (or through our resources), Miranda, did the Lord teach you during this trial?

There were so many things that I learned through the Word of the God once I found my way here.

To pray, to fast, to forgive, to speak only what is necessary, remain quiet, to always obey the Lord and to give everything in prayer to Him, to be submissive to my earthly husband (something I never imagined having to do, because no one had ever taught me this), working at home and taking care of our family (another thing I did not know and had never heard of in my life), even though I work outside the home, I have already given it to God to do his will. And so many other wonderful teachings that only the Lord could teach me through His Word given to me by RMI, on the RMI site (which I thank the Lord for having sent me here). And every day I learn more and more.

What were the most difficult times that God helped you through Miranda?

The hardest moment for me was when I discovered the utter betrayal; when my earthly husband told me, he did not love me anymore and that he wanted to leave me. The scorn and humiliation I went through God brought me through. Also, when I found out that my husband had lied that he was going to work on my birthday and instead went to be with the OW and I called, and she answered.

All these moments the Lord carried me, comforted me on His lap and in truth I do not know what would have become of me if he had not done it for me, because my hope of living was over. If it were not for finding my way here, I would have taken my own life.

Miranda, what was the "turning point" of your restoration?

It was when I asked the Lord and my earthly husband for forgiveness for everything I had done. Next was when I stopped speaking everything that came to my mind and instead applied the principle to "win without words" as this applies to everything not just winning a husband. Also, each time I let it go, I saw things turn around. Oh, and the biggest changes occurred the moment I stopped giving my *tithe* to the Local church and I started to give it to RMI (my treasure house) where I am spiritually fed. Don't expect changes to happen until you *surrender and trust Him.*

Tell us HOW it happened Miranda? Did your husband just walk in the front door? Miranda, did you suspect or could you tell you were close to being restored?

My husband, by God's grace, never left our home, even though he was with an OW. The day he was going to go to his mother's house, he gave up and could not go. And I know that it was the Lord who inclined his heart and did not let him leave the house.

So, I just have to thank the Lord again for everything He has done and is doing in my family, because what God has joined man does not separate. I will be forever grateful to the Lord for the rest of my life for everything He's done and will continue to do as long as He is first.

Would you recommend any of our resource in particular that helped you Miranda?

I recommend every single resource offered by RMI. Each is wonderful and speaks to everything you are or will be going through. Don't stop with just the first book and first course. Continue your journey if you truly want restoration. Remember, each book and video are the Word of the Lord, His message. What He wants you to know in order to give you the abundant life.

Begin with the *testimonies* books; then read the book *How God Can and Will Restore Your Marriage*, do the *courses*; wake up to the *Encourager* and do the courses a second time in the evening instead of watching TV. Don't miss the book *A Wise Woman* and then continue to live *abundantly* by taking these new courses offered in order to truly make the Lord your HH.

Would you be interested in helping encourage other women Miranda?

Yes

Either way Miranda, what kind of encouragement would you like to leave women with, in conclusion?

I ask each of you who are reading my testimony to never give up. When the fight gets heavier than you can bare remember that it's His battle. And when God comes in He will change the whole story. Just as He changed mine, He will change yours as well and you will be writing your own testimony.

UPDATE: Hello RMI. We were blessed with another son and wanted to send a new family picture.

Chapter 13

Ariela

"I am the Lord, the God of all mankind.
Is anything too hard for me?"
—Jeremiah 32:27

"One Year 'It is Over, Period.'"

Ariela, how did your restoration actually begin?

It began just two weeks before we had been married for only a year. On Monday morning my husband went to work, and he never came home. I called his work and they said he hadn't come in, that he had called and asked to cancel all his appointments, that he would not be in that day. So that's when I started to call his cell phone, but he wouldn't answer. The next afternoon I had a doctor's appointment, but I couldn't stop worrying because he had disappeared, he was not answering his phone, not coming in to work for the second day.

When I returned home I found the biggest shock of my life! He had come home when I was gone and took everything! That's when I stopped worrying and became angry!! The very next day I got a call from his lawyer saying that he wanted a divorce and that I was to go to his office, that he would answer all the questions I had and that my husband would have no further contact with me!

So, I started to send text message after text message, but he would not answer me. To make me stop, he began sending me the same message, "It is over, period."

Then I was given the book How God Can and Will Restore Your Marriage from a person I didn't even know. That's when I found this life-changing ministry. I was so blessed! I started to read this book and then read the two Facing Divorce books were sent to me when I filled out the Marriage Evaluation Questionnaire. It was then that the Lord showed me that this tragedy had happened so that I could turn to Him and put Him first. That this was not a marriage crisis, it was only for the purpose of my finding my HH and my abundant life that everything happened.

I began to praise Him and that's when my first miracle happened. On our marriage anniversary, which I had forgotten about because I was being pampered by my HH, my husband sent me a message at midnight wishing me a happy birthday (we got married on my birthday). This was after only speaking through his lawyer for months and being told, "It is over, period." But God writes the last chapter when we put Him first.

How did God change your situation Ariela as you sought Him wholeheartedly?

So, I started to follow the principles of the book, and in fact, everything in this book and Facing Divorce is what God really wants to teach all of us. It's insane because I had talked to several pastors who all told me to separate and move on. That God had someone better. Many told me because I'm too young to live as a single woman, to hire a good lawyer, to follow what I wanted for my life. But by really beginning to know His Word, after hungering for it once I found RMI and your resources, I began to understand that God did not want anything close to this! He wanted to restore my marriage. Then I became so intimate of my Beloved Lord, my HH, and He was with me. Any time I felt anxious, He began telling me that I was to wait on Him, to calm down because my husband would return. I embraced myself in these words of my Lord and let nothing else disturb me. I went ahead on my journey with my HH and followed each of the principles shared in your books.

What principles, from God's Word (or through our resources), Ariela, did the Lord teach you during this trial?

I understood that I had to be submissive to my husband so that the word of God would not be blasphemed. I needed a meek, gentle and quiet spirit, and I could no longer be that "contentious woman" I'd been. Confronting and always contradictory, I needed to love and submit to my husband, for it would please my Beloved Lord and it's He who needed to be first in my life. So, I began to fast and pray intensely for intimacy with my Lord and soon He was all I wanted, needed and longed for.

What were the most difficult times that God helped you through Ariela?

Sometimes the enemy wanted to confuse me, and he'd bring people to speak words and muddy my thoughts, saying that my restoration might just be an idea I dreamed up in my head. So, I am grateful to my HH, the love of my life who held me and comforted me and answered every question I had. No matter how many times I asked, He answered me with all the verses I'd sown in my heart by reading the stack of 3x5 cards I'd written and read when I was desperate to stop the pain.

Ariela, what was the "turning point" of your restoration?

The turning point was when I understood the purposes of the Lord for me, that is, to be the bride for Him, for me to want Him again and to embrace Him as my true Husband and believe that He is Lord. "I am the Lord, the God of all mankind. Is there anything difficult for me?" Jeremiah 32:27.

Tell us HOW it happened Ariela? Did your husband just walk in the front door? Ariela, did you suspect or could you tell you were close to being restored?

Miraculously, after two months and two years without seeing or even talking to my husband, we met again.

How this occurred was supernatural. I heard the same word for 6 days. The word was "Why are you crying out to Me? ...go forward." It was on the seventh day that I sensed something was about to end. Then I stood up with the strongest feeling that I should go out, not knowing where I was going. So, I put on some clothes and I left without understanding why, and just as I was crossing the street to go to a friend's house, I noticed that my husband was stopped, just sitting in the car across the street watching me as I walked. At just that moment, I received a phone call, a returned phone message from someone I'd called earlier that morning, but when I looked down, he drove off. As he drove off, I looked at the car, but then I really wasn't sure it was actually him. I tried but I could not read the license plate.

So, I kept walking but then I heard His voice say, "Turn around, go back there," but I was confused. I turned around and went back but I started crying right there in the middle of the street. Then I spotted his car again and felt kind of impelled to walk towards the car. When I arrived, I saw he was in there, but he had the windows shut. When he looked at me, he lowered the window, and reached out to take my hand. Then he asked me to get in the car.

It was all so beautiful what the Lord did, we embraced for a few minutes without saying one word. God acted miraculously on my behalf. I would like to make it clear that my marriage was restored even without having children. I was so worried it wasn't possible. Hallelujah!

Would you recommend any of our resource in particular that helped you Ariela?

I recommend to all the women who are going through the same desert that I have come through to read the book *How God Can and Will Restore Your Marriage*. Oh, how precious it was to me when someone I didn't even know gave this book to me. Dear friend, it was by the grace and mercy of the Lord that your resources helped me as I went through my journey of restoration. Thank you.

What crystallized the principles was when I took your *courses*. Journaling is something I did from the beginning but having a form and an email to reread helped me a lot to see how much He was changing me. I'd also encourage everyone to take time to make 3x5 cards and read them all the time.

Actually, what is first, is the restoration with Him, and once He is first, and that's when the restoration of your marriage will happen. I have already been able to bless so many lives by giving this book, so they could read and be blessed as I was. I think I've already purchased 3 *cases of 25* so far and have given them out.

Would you be interested in helping encourage other women Ariela?

Yes

Either way Ariela, what kind of encouragement would you like to leave women with, in conclusion?

Today I only have to thank and glorify my Lord, my Beloved HH, for having first brought me again to have an intimacy with Him. Next is the miracle of having my husband back in my life, living at home with me as husband and wife. And may I tell each of you, do not give up on your marriage, because with God there is nothing impossible or even faintly difficult for Him. He is greater than anything you face, so stop doing it on your own in your own way. Your journey has been carefully mapped out by God through this ministry. Just follow Him who led you here, and just believe—your miracle will happen!

Chapter 14

Kadison

"If you remain in me and
my words remain in you,
ask whatever you wish,
and it will be done for you."
—John 15:7

"I Felt Dirty for What I Had Done"

Kadison, how did your restoration actually begin?

It began a day soon after I found out I was expecting our 2nd son, and I noticed that my husband started behaving differently. I always had his passwords for everything, mostly because we worked together in my father-in-law's company and used social networks for business. But then, after I had our second child, I left my father-in-law's company and started working at home.

One day, I saw that he had added an old friend who worked where he worked when he was just 18 and then I noticed a few days later that he'd changed all his passwords. Well, I became suspicious, jealous, so I started to search his cell phone. That's when my world collapsed! I found what I did not want to believe. I saw he had an OW. I sent a message and cursed the OW, but that only made things much worse.

I sought advice from single friends who all encouraged me to separate, give myself some time alone, be apart, but those things were what I wanted to hear. Foolishly it was what I did— I sent him away. Told him to leave. Oh, there was so much heartache, and despite his ongoing involvement with the OW and me cursing her, my husband did not abandon me.

Even more amazing is that even though I was prepared to give birth to my son alone, when our son born, my husband was there during the entire labor and childbirth. He stayed with me and took care of both of us in the first days after we got home—even though I'd kicked him out.

Of course, I regretted what I had done, and right away I began to beg for his love. But this complete change only served to suffocate him. I begged for his forgiveness, pleaded with him to come back over and over again. Then when he didn't return, I flipped again and forbade him to see his children. I did so many horrible things that I am ashamed to speak of today (I'm sorry they're just too horrible). I took more advice from "friends" and said that I did not love him anymore, and that when he came over he would need supervised visitation. Either I or a mediator would need to be present if he wanted to see his children. Well, that caused me many sleepless nights, extreme weight loss, and worse, I became a bitter, ugly woman. Then I told him I just wanted both of us "to be happy" in other words, let's just move on. What another huge mistake!!

How did God change your situation Kadison as you sought Him wholeheartedly?

On one of those sleepless nights, I began to search the internet for marriage stories, testimonies, etc. ... and by Divine Appointment I found RMI. The moment I read the first page on HopeAtLast.com it was as if scales fell from my eyes!!! That night I returned to the ways of the Lord with an interest in Him again. I finally had hope; hope that one day my family and I would be restored. I first discovered what having a Father was like. A Father who was full of love and infinite mercy, who gradually restored my broken heart, bringing me to a place of understanding. A Father who began showing me what was wrong in my life and leading me along a path of peace. He spoke to me about entering a 30-day fast, to know what the will of God was, and to discover His will, not mine.

Dear brides, in just 10 days, during a service, a sister I did not know came to me through His leading and revealed to me that God saw my tears and that He was taking care of me and my children and told me that I should not give up on my dreams. I was in shock, I had NEVER seen that woman! Well, I finished the 30-day fast, but nothing really changed. I'd been waiting all year, waiting on the Lord, then I became very ill, and while on the internet I had a horrible relapse, going back to my old ways.

I'd let go of Facebook but in my weakness, I went on when an ex-boyfriend contacted me. We got together and afterward, I felt dirty for what I had done. The Lord had promised me, my family so much. He took care of me, gave me a great job, so what was I doing?! This is what I thought after I fell...But God is merciful and does not fail us when we fail Him. He forgave me, picked me up, and introduced me to His Son who needed to be my Heavenly Husband to rid me of any sort of temptation like that again.

What principles, from God's Word (or through our resources), Kadison, did the Lord teach you during this trial?

The reading of the Word of God must be our main food, only in God will we find refuge. And if we fill ourselves with spiritual junk food, we will be sick. We must feed from the pure water of His Word and help ourselves overcome by remaining encouraged through testimonies.

Leaving the church is extremely important, wow, it makes ALL the difference. Yet after, even during LEAVING, it is very necessary to find and embrace your HH.

NEVER speak evil about your husband to anyone, leave his part of the closet empty, and speak blessings on your home and your family by smiling at the future. It's not what you see or how you feel, but what you are hoping for against all hope.

What were the most difficult times that God helped you through Kadison?

Though I first found the Father I never had growing up, it was having a HH that sustained me when my husband simply disappeared for six months, without telling anyone. Later we found out he had only communicated with his mother and asked about the children through her. But she also did not hear from him many months. Had I believed my earthly husband to be who I longed for, I know my life would have been unbearable. Instead, though, I had a HH and a Father for my children. I was well loved, entirely cared for in every way. I glowed, and my children thrived.

Kadison, what was the "turning point" of your restoration?

The turning point was the day my brother-in-law came over to talk to me. He told me that my husband wanted to get closer to me, but that he did not know how, because he was living with this OW. He said he wanted to come home but knew I had LET him GO. He told my brother-in-law that he loved me, and he missed our family and had heard from everyone that I had become a virtuous woman.

Tell us HOW it happened Kadison? Did your husband just walk in the front door? Kadison, did you suspect or could you tell you were close to being restored?

The month after my brother-in-law came over to talk to me, my husband came to visit the children and at the end of the day, before leaving, he said he wanted to talk to me. He said that he had NEVER stopped loving me and that if I allowed him, he would come back and be forever faithful. We kissed again after almost 3 years. I could not believe what was happening and only managed to smile, my heart was beating so fast. I could tell his heart was beating fast too, and that day, maybe for the first time, we fell in love. That was eight months ago and each day we feel the same thing when we kiss.

We've structured our lives entirely around the Lord. He is at the center, each of us keeps Him as our first Love. Once home, he began to renovate our apartment, and the biggest change is that he wants to stay home to be with me and the kids all the time. This time together resulted in us expecting a restoration baby, a girl, who is due in less than two months.

Yes, I know the enemy continues to come against us, but the Lord, my HH, is with me. And I will never leave Him again, for, without His presence, I would surely die ... there is no life in me without the Lord as my HH.

Would you recommend any of our resource in particular that helped you Kadison?

I recommend to ALL the people I meet, anyone who goes through anything like this, to read my testimony. I already sent it to several friends. One friend of mine used the resources of RM that I bought her, and a few months later I heard that she also had her marriage restored! This is my ministry, to continue to accompany you, Erin, and in order to thank you for helping us in a moment where the world told us to give up. My ministry is to reach out, share my testimony, boast about my weaknesses, in order that He can use me to speak about finding Him as my HH and to share and purchase resources as my offering (my tithe goes here).

Dear sister, if you want what I have, you just need to believe in your Divine Appointment and then promise Him, as I did, that if He will restore you that you will help others in a marriage crisis—forever, glorifying God for the rest your life with the testimony He wants to give you.

Maybe that's why restoration doesn't always stick, because once He's given, so few give back to Him by sharing what He did for them.

Would you be interested in helping encourage other women Kadison?

Yes, always and forever!

Either way Kadison, what kind of encouragement would you like to leave women with, in conclusion?

If every woman knew what God has for her marriage and her family, if everyone tried to see the heart of God, divorces would not exist, so many traumas in life would be avoided. So, my sister, my brother, just believe, be willing to speak His truth and give Hope to others. If you do, GOD WILL RESTORE YOUR FAMILY, in the name of Jesus ... He is with you right now... talk to Him, tell Him this is what you want.

"If you abide in Me, and My words abide in you, ask whatever you wish, and it shall be done for you" (John 15:7). Just as Erin says, when your heart rests in Him alone and your will is centered in His will, you are truly making Him Lord. To know His will is to know His Word. It is His will that your marriage be healed. He hates divorce, and we are to be reconciled; however, He has conditions. Make Him first. Find your HH.

Chapter 15

Nicolle

"Then you will know the truth,
and the truth will set you free."
—John 8:32

"His Truth Liberates and Transforms Me"

Nicolle, how did your restoration actually begin?

Today I am here to speak of the goodness and mercy of the Lord in my life and the restoration of my marriage.

In November, six years ago, I discovered that I was pregnant after eight years of dating my boyfriend. I was very excited about the pregnancy, so I told my boyfriend, who at the time lived and worked in another city quite far from me.

When I was five months pregnant my boyfriend got the transfer to move to our city. That's when we started planning to get married and move to our new apartment. That's when the fighting between us became intense. We fought over everything, but the biggest argument was about him converting and becoming a Catholic. He did not want to marry into a religion that was not his. Even with the fights, we eventually married and a month later I had my son.

Four months after my son was born I began to realize that my husband was very distant and cold towards me. He had zero patience with me. In the face of the situation I began to question the reason for his coldness. He claimed that he was still very hurt because I was relentless, and I forced him to marry into a religion that was not his. He said he'd told me (which he had) that he preferred us to live together without marrying and that he'd married me out of force.

Very soon I discovered that he had an OW in the city where he once worked and that even after he married me, he often traveled to meet and be with her. At that moment I really was focused, so I asked him to just leave the house, but while he packed his bags I was talking to God. Soon after he asked me if this was really what I wanted, so I said no, he could stay in our home until we resolved our situation. It was a very difficult time for me, a time of fear, of oppression, of despair, of insecurity, of questioning everything.

How did God change your situation Nicolle as you sought Him wholeheartedly?

In August of that same year, my sister told me about the marriage testimony of a singer she liked. During the research, I found RMI and the book *How God Can and Will Restore Your Marriage*. At that moment it was a new beginning for me! Prior to finding this book I was aimless, without direction, and God began to guide me on the path I was to follow.

With the book, the testimonies, the praise reports and the daily reading of the Bible when I purchased the *reading through the Bible*, I began to surrender to God. That's when He revealed my sins. I could never live a happy life without being set free before he restored my marriage, and our crisis was what God used to reach me, heal me, and set me free. When I was dating I was always quarrelsome, spiteful, and argumentative. I wanted to be the man of the relationship, being bossy, and honestly, so ridiculous in my superior attitude.

Besides how I acted towards everyone, I was simply a lukewarm believer who went to church only on Sundays. I did not read the Bible, I had no fellowship or relationship with God and only partly acknowledged His Son as my Savior. I was insecure, I needed constant affirmation. I did not think I was a nice person, and I thought a lot about other people's opinions of who I was or what I should do. There was no way I would ever be a virtuous woman. Not until I met my one true Love.

What principles, from God's Word (or through our resources), Nicolle, did the Lord teach you during this trial?

There were so many, but I guess it's when I began to focus on God and found my Husband. I immediately stopped telling people about my situation with my husband, I stayed home for the first time in my life. I spent time praying and reading the Bible. I believe in just a couple of months I'd read it through the entire Bible 3 times using my app (listening and reading). The transformation was amazing. I didn't even look the same and I certainly didn't act the same way. People took notice and I began being complimented. But people's opinions no longer mattered to me. There was only one Person who I cared about. The One who'd loved me unconditionally.

What were the most difficult times that God helped you through Nicolle?

When my husband traveled, and I stayed at home with our baby son, I knew where he was going so at first it really bothered me. From the beginning, my earthly husband did not care about me, about us, but once I got past allowing my mind to think of these things, He began to lessen the burden I had been feeling. There's no doubt that without Him and His love, without spending as much time as I did reading through the Bible, without RMI's resources guiding me I know I would have created a scandal and done something I'd have to live with now that I'm restored.

Nicolle, what was the "turning point" of your restoration?

The moment I started to apply letting go, and I fell in love with my *HH*. Almost instantly my husband started looking for me. My HH would take me and the baby out for long walks and he'd come looking for me. Once my heart was His, my husband was no longer cold towards me anymore. There was no more tension in the air when he'd come home from work.

Another turning point might have been what happened the month before my restoration. I experienced a very painful ordeal meant to destroy me. Though I thought I could not take it, my *HH* supported me and we came through it even closer. Immediately afterwards, restoration happened.

Tell us HOW it happened Nicolle? Did your husband just walk in the front door? Nicolle, did you suspect or could you tell you were close to being restored?

In January, my husband called me, saying he had to talk. He finally told me about the OW (even though I'd known about her for months but wisely said nothing). He told me how horrible he'd felt each time he was with the OW and finally had put an end to it. He said he was sorry for everything, that he would understand if I did not want to forgive him. He said he was enjoying his married life and wanted to continue it with me, remaining faithful to me, if I was willing.

Although I had heard some things I did not want to hear that day, I felt relieved he'd confessed, because the cord that once existed was broken that day. We started to get right from that day forward.

As Erin says, there are still many things God will put in place in our lives as a couple. There's still a journey up ahead, but it will all happen by God's grace and in His timing. Our marriage is nothing like it was, it's new, different, still with challenges but so much better than I'd ever imagined it could be.

Would you recommend any of our resource in particular that helped you Nicolle?

I recommend the all the *books,* videos and *courses* from this ministry. I'd also encourage everyone to continue reading the daily *praise reports* because they will keep you encouraged and you'll need the encouragement. I'd especially recommend *reading through the Bible* using the *Alexandar Scourby* app. Make it your new routine, reading the bible every day: morning, noon and night. Just never stop doing the daily reading.

Stop your social life and wasting this time He's given you. Allow God to give you a makeover. Honestly, if it were not for finding RMI and being guided by this ministry, without a doubt I would still be doing everything wrong and reaping the consequences. The principles all work together, so when you omit or skip one you'll find yourself not seeing your journey moving forward. Trust the path provided for you and don't try to take shortcuts.

Would you be interested in helping encourage other women Nicolle?

Yes

Either way Nicolle, what kind of encouragement would you like to leave women with, in conclusion?

Today I know how important it is to build the family on the Rock that is Him and His Word. How important it is to pray, to fast, and to watch for Him to lead us along our journey. There's a real enemy who seeks to swallow families and destroy them. But most important for all of us to remember is that GOD will restore. He has already won everything for us on the cross of Calvary. God loves us and is crying out for us to meet and love His Son.

He says, "Call unto me, and I will answer thee, and shew thee great and mighty things, which thou knowest not." Jeremiah 33:3.

Beloved, let us not stand still waiting for our families to be destroyed. God has left us His Word, His Word that will guide, heal us and transform us and our families. We must meditate, recite and take possession of every promise that is in the scriptures.

Cry out with all your heart and give yourself to Him and the more He will do seeing He is first.

I am being treated in all areas of my life with respect, with love all because I sought God to restore my marriage. Then with all my soul, with all my heart, and with all my understanding I put my Husband first.

Today I know that I am loved, that I all I dreamed did come true. I am His beautiful bride.

I thank God especially for His kindness, His mercy and His infinite love for me and mostly for the *HH* who cherishes me. I thank Him for every praise report I read, and to everyone who is part of the RMI team. I especially thank Erin, because it was through this ministry that I was able to truly know His truth that liberates and transforms me.

Live the supernatural life as His bride. Praise the Lord in the most difficult moments of your life, thank Him for your victory even before you see it. Do not forget that everything has already been overcome by the blood of the Lamb and the word of our testimony. Share the truth of what God is doing with others, share the love He's shown you with others. Take possession of what is yours, His love, His future. Do not think about the past and stop looking at the waves of the sea. Keep your eyes fixed on Him.

Chapter 16

Vanessa

"...Call on me in the day of trouble;
I will deliver you, and you will honor me."
—Psalm 50:15

"Celebrating our Son's Birthday He Introduced Me as his Wife"

Vanessa, how did your restoration actually begin?

I was completely lost, trying to find sense in my life. I felt rejected and was full of shame, so I tried to run away from everything —working, making money and also leaving my hometown, so I could be far from the shameful memories that made me feel sick :(

In the midst of so much despair and fear, I looked at my son, and I began to cry out for more of God and His help to get out of this situation. That's when I found RMI on the internet, it was such a light to me, I really feel so very grateful!

I guess it all started at the very beginning of our marriage, as we didn't know each other very well. Actually, we met, got engaged and married in only 10 months and one of my greatest fears happened: one month after our marriage, I became pregnant.

My husband and I didn't have any kind of support or example from our families. Both of us were living with unsolved problems and very heavy emotional baggage that we brought to our marriage.

Being pregnant led me to emotional crisis. My EH didn't know what to do or how to deal with a brand-new wife, a wife who was now pregnant. By this time, there were a lot of people counseling us, mainly the pastor of the church we used to attend together. He did in an isolated way, I mean, he never talked with the both of us at the same time, as a couple, he always talked to us separately.

I complained about his methods to my husband, but since he admired him so much, it was like my EH put him on a pedestal, so everything I said seemed to be against me. We just quarreled about all of this!

As time went by, things began to get worse :(We were living in a rented place, and there were a lot of things happening, all the same things many of the ladies tell us about here in our ministry. First of all, we left the church. Then we preferred being with friends instead of being with each other or our family and there were a lot of quarrels in the process. Finally, unemployment hit us, and we had to go live in my parents' house. This is when we separated.

As I didn't have any kind of instruction nor wisdom, I didn't know what to do or how to act and react even when I was doing something right. On the other hand, there were a lot of problems and lack of wisdom, I received "help" from my family, encouraging misconduct and separation.

How did God change your situation Vanessa as you sought Him wholeheartedly?

I knew that there were a lot of bad and wrong actions and feelings in me, and there was also the lack of wisdom and an emotional imbalance. At that time, all those things together made me decide, agreeing with my EH, that the best thing to do was to ask him to leave our home. By this time, we accepted the sentence of separation ... yet, that's when my transforming began.

It was the day I really saw myself alone, with a newborn baby to whom my EH used to say he loved more than life, but he was not there anymore. Now he was with other people, living his life with his job. I stood before God and opened my heart with all the strength I had at that moment. I cried for days and days, but I presented myself completely to the Lord.

So, I sensed that I was being transformed, getting closer to Him, facing my mistakes, and being released from my physical and emotional traumas. Soon the Holy Spirit guided me through the tears to find the RMI, and it was the most beautiful prayer response I received that my life changed. Then I saw that it was God's will, and not just mine, to restore the marriage that He gave me as a gift. Yes, my wedding was a gift – and now I knew!

With the help of RMI, I could see that much of what I had done until I found this ministry was right. Things like when I was led to ask for forgiveness, to give my troubles to God, and especially to allow Him to really, fully and deeply change me. And also, that I had recognized my mistakes and failures.

I had been a very bad person, quarrelsome, disrespectful, hurtful, yet wounded, proud, full of vanity, and I could not give genuine forgiveness to anyone. And in everything, God was working, and He keeps on doing so, everything is happening in His perfect timing.

Soon I could see myself in a lighter, happier life, with another vision for my future and a new heart. I have seen everything begin to make sense, I have really seen what it is to love and be with my Heavenly Husband. And I started to live one day after another joyfully. Soon, I began to live the abundant life and receive the daily miracles that my Beloved has for me and my family.

What principles, from God's Word (or through our resources), Vanessa, did the Lord teach you during this trial?

The Lord taught me and confirmed all the principles I learned here at RMI. If it were not for these teachings, I would not have been able to go far in my journey and to be here today, living the best time of my life! Being meek and gentle helped me a lot to get rid of the bad feelings that I had, concerning my EH.

Letting go of the church was the best thing I did, because I became totally dependent on the Lord and totally close to Him alone. This helped me to fix my mistake of making church my spiritual leader.

Moving away from social networks helped a lot during those very hard days—this was very effective. It helped me to be free from the pain that I had created when I saw something that had the power to hurt me by believing in something that did not really exist.

To let go, definitely was the best of all, because it was when I really became a totally happy and loved woman. At that time my EH was living in another state with a friend, and I was living a very happy life as His bride :) It was and still is an incredible time after I was able to let go for real.

What were the most difficult times that God helped you through Vanessa?

The entire time was very hard! When you have feelings for someone else, it's easy to feel hurt at being apart. But the moments that struck me the most, were the days I saw myself in the hospital with my sick baby, also when I saw a framed photo of my EH with an OW - no doubt that was the worst day! Then when his "friends" came along just to give me "news", but I could feel the love of the Lord sustaining me.

There were also financial issues that the Lord helped me through a lot—infinitely surprising me and saving me in every situation, and even today, He keeps on moving in my favor.

Vanessa, what was the "turning point" of your restoration?

The turning point was when I truly let go and became happy and in love with my Heavenly Husband.

At that exact time, my EH began to talk to me and began approaching. We began to have a relationship as friends again. Amazingly, I began to experience good dreams, dreams that were becoming true.

I also received the gift of being part of a team that I love so very much, and I have them as dear friends. Here on our Portuguese Ministry Team!!

Tell us HOW it happened Vanessa? Did your husband just walk in the front door? Vanessa, did you suspect or could you tell you were close to being restored?

Well, I did not suspect it would be so soon—even though I could see the signs. Then came the month of our son's birthday, and my EH said he would come, because he had to work with some colleagues. He also said he would not be able to arrive as soon as he would like to do. At that time, we were closer, friends again, some issues from our past had been solved. Sometimes he would declare himself in small sentences and say that he missed us as a family and missed me as his wife.

When he arrived in our state, he stayed in another city and we talked for as long as possible. At that moment, he opened his heart telling me of his dreams and wishes for our family. He said how much he was thinking about me and us together again and that he wanted to get here soon ... When he arrived in our city, he surprised me! He phoned me when he was at our front door, he said: "I arrived, I'm here"! I felt like a young girl in love again!

At that moment, there was no room for anything from the past, only the Love of God among us. I opened the door and my heart started pounding, because it was too surprising for me, for the first time after 1 year and 8 months, I was near him and I could hug him like my EH.

Since then, God has restored our family. The next day we went out to celebrate our son's birthday and for the first time after this long period of time, he introduced me as his wife.

While he was here, we stayed all together at my mother-in-law's house, because I was living in my parents' house. But soon he needed to go back to where he was living and working. At that moment I had the full certainty that God had given me a rest - a "Selah" - to be prepared for what was to happen.

One month later and totally by surprise, my EH came back to live in our city :) He is considering us a family again, calling me "his wife" and wishing our family together. And within a few months, he changed the status of his Facebook page to "married" again and he is using our pictures. We have also returned to being husband and wife as it should be after so long. God answered our prayers!!

I believe that soon, very soon, we will be living in our own house, not with relatives, and giving much more value to our home and family! Then I will have a new testimony to share with you :)

Would you recommend any of our resource in particular that helped you Vanessa?

I recommend all the materials! Use as many as you can and get as much as the Lord gives you and retain as much knowledge as possible!

In particular, the book **How God Can and Will Restore Your Marriage**, and the *Be Encouraged videos*, using the lessons for our *online courses,* and absorb the encouragement in our *Daily Encourager* in a daily basis :)

Would you be interested in helping encourage other women Vanessa?

Yes!!!! It will be a great joy to be able to help more and more., as I'm already part of the Portuguese Team!

Either way Vanessa, what kind of encouragement would you like to leave women with, in conclusion?

Beloved brides, I know it is a painful time at first, but keep on going! Do not give up!

Go forward and cling to the Lord, truly let go of everything else, for thus you will discover the true happiness and love that our Beloved yearns to share with us all the days of our lives.

And it does not matter what you see and hear, ignore this and give yourself fully to Him and rest. For God has all the power to restore and He will ... He has done this for me and is still doing so and He will also do the same for you!!

Open your heart and let HIM in, let Him transform you completely and then you will see your life completely transformed for better—much more than you could imagine!

Chapter 17

Willow

"His own iniquities will capture the wicked,
And he will be held with the cords of his sin"
—Proverbs 5:22

"OW Beat Him Badly"

Willow, how did your restoration actually begin?

Hello! Grace and peace! I almost submitted my restored marriage testimony when my husband first came home, but because he continued to correspond on WhatsApp with OW and I knew he sometimes went to find her because she lives in another state, I decided to wait until God had completed this last part of my restoration journey. And HE did!!!

How did God change your situation Willow as you sought Him wholeheartedly?

After my husband came home, since his heart was still for the OW, I continued to apply the principles that Erin teaches, such as letting go and winning without words. I continued unceasingly seeking to improve my relationship with my *HH*. I found our *Love Song*, and told Him over and over how He was all I needed and wanted. I asked Him (like Michele suggests in *Finding your Abundant Life*) how we could get closer (me and Him) and sure enough, I began to fall deeply for my *HH*. No longer did I long, or need, or was desperate for my EH to get rid of the OW. What I did want was for him, for my EH, to be broken from the cords of his sin. "His own iniquities will capture the wicked, and he will be held with the cords of his sin"—Proverbs 5:22 But I no longer wanted it for my benefit. How He went about this was nothing I expected would happen!

What principles, from God's Word (or through our resources), Willow, did the Lord teach you during this trial?

I learned that I needed to depend on God to be transformed, to give me my_*makeover* and that only God is who will turn the heart. I learned my EH's heart will not turn towards me until God knows my heart was for my *HH* and my relationship with Him remains first. If we yearn, long, talk about and are obsessed with our marriage restoration and our husbands, God will continue to make us a loathing to them. Above all, I have learned to trust God with my future, to my *Husband*, alone.

What were the most difficult times that God helped you through Willow?

The most difficult moment was when I discovered a profile of him with the OW on facebook. He had already come home, and many close friends knew that he was at home. But with that profile of him on facebook with OW it made me look like a fool for praising God for my restoration. It was clearly the enemy trying to take me down, make me stumble horribly. If I had not reactivated my facebook account, and followed the principle to create a new FB with my *BNN* and begin to focus on ministering to hurting women, like the hurting woman I once was, I would not have seen it. Thankfully God quickly forgave me and gave me the grace to overcome! The hurt was gone and my faith renewed when I followed what it says, made my *BNN* FB and began reaching out to women who were hurting, sending them to *HopeAtLast.com* to encourage them to follow their own Restoration Journey.

Willow, what was the "turning point" of your restoration?

The turning point I believe was the perseverance in following the principles like I just mentioned. I also believe it was once I really began believing in God and knowing that HE began the good work, therefore, HE would complete it, regardless of any circumstances that presented themselves! And as long as my HH was first, and I was reaching out and focusing on others, not myself, soon, very soon this last part of my restoration would be complete. And it was!

Tell us HOW it happened Willow? Did your husband just walk in the front door? Willow, did you suspect or could you tell you were close to being restored?

About six months ago, my husband contacted me, saying that he wanted to return home to be with me. And although he has remained home since that time, and said and showed me that he loved me, I sensed he had not fully let go of the OW.

One day he came to me crying. Since coming home, he had asked me to pray all the time. This time he was asking, begging, that God would break the strong ties he was constantly fighting to go back to the OW, even though, he said in his heart he didn't want to. He even asked me to go to a new church with him.

Then one weekend he up and left to meet with OW. The OW is from another state. Several hours later he contacted me through a cell phone message. He said he needed help. He said he and the OW had disagreed and she beat him badly. He said he contacted his family to get help but they were angry and would not come. So he asked me to help by contacting 2 brothers from the new church, to see if they could go get him. I had no idea how bad it was, not until he arrived. When I met him at the hospital, he had a broken jaw and cuts all over his face. While at the hospital he asked me for forgiveness. He also accepted the visits from many members (including the pastor) who can from the church. There is no doubt that now he is truly broken and wants nothing to do with the OW or any OW. He said he has a real fear of God now and wants the kind of relationship he's witnessed in me!

Would you recommend any of our resource in particular that helped you Willow?

I recommend *HopeAtLast.com* to everyone and also to purchase the paperback book *How God Can and Will Restore Your Marriage*. I suggest everyone read the *Daily Encourager* and follow your free *courses* offered on the RMI Website.

Would you be interested in helping encourage other women Willow?

YES

Either way Willow, what kind of encouragement would you like to leave women with, in conclusion?

God is Faithful! He changes the course of the universe when you decide to let Him fight for you. Once you make your *HH* first, begin to focus on helping other women, and give Him time to work—trust that God works miracles, restoration will happen! He can turn the murky waters of your life into fine wine! As long you strictly obey the Word, follow the principles, there's no reason victory will not come to you. Without a doubt anything with God is possible! God guarantees what He says in His Word!

Chapter 18

Betha

"And we know that in all things God works
for the good of those who love him, who
have been called according to his purpose."
—Romans 8:28

"Almost 2 Months not Wanting to See our Daughter"

Betha, how did your restoration actually begin?

Good afternoon my loved ones. My journey all started on Christmas almost ten years ago when I discovered my husband's first betrayal. I kicked him out of the house, then he repented but I decided NOT to forgive him. In the middle of the next month, I discovered that I was pregnant, so we agreed to give our marriage a go. I found out I was pregnant the day after I had already told him that I hated him. I also said in that heated argument that I did not want to forgive him. I thought that forgiveness was about a feeling I would have. But forgiveness is not a feeling! I learned the very hard lesson that forgiveness is a decision we choose to make because it is His command to us as believers.

I also learned that the Lord yearned for me, and my BELOVED is jealous of my time. Sometimes, He just wanted me to spend time alone with Him. Since I was so involved in myself, because we as humans are selfish, it was through this long journey I discovered this truth and even more I never knew about.

Even though I was born into a Christian evangelical home and I am the daughter of pastors who both ministers. Yet as I was getting settled into married life, I forgot how I once lived and so much that I was never taught. I lived through so many beautiful times with my Beloved, so many experiences spending time in nature with Him. Yet, once married,

I simply did not want to make time for Him and certainly not seeking a deeper intimacy with Him. I moved away from His promises and I began to live with a heart full of strength (the way women in the world are taught to be). And like the world, I chose not to forgive either my earthly husband nor my Beloved for allowing this betrayal.

Since I no longer believed the man in my life loved me, God got my attention. A year later I was given a large financial Inheritance that the Lord entrusted to me (even without me deserving it). Soon after I got very sick and almost lost the inheritance because the money was needed to pay for me to regain my life after being so horribly ill for so long. These were days of endless, intense pain.

Then as everyone who is chosen of God, I returned to the ways of the Lord and the Lord is so gracious that He embraced me fully. But not even all I went through brought me closer to the Lord, not really. It was all due to me, I still did not forgive the Lord for allowing me to suffer so much, first betrayal and then my sickness! I did not understand that all that He allowed me to pass through was so that His name would be glorified and I should be transformed into who I needed to be.

Soon after our baby's arrival, we agreed to raise our daughter in the way of the Lord, so we sought a good church and became members. That's when I saw clearly that my husband was no longer the same man as he once was. My husband began serving the Lord with so much passion and enthusiasm. Yet, as far as I was concerned, just as the Word itself says, "The wise woman builds her house and the fool destroys it with her own hands." This is what happened for 7 horrible years— I was destroying a marriage that was practically perfect. I had a wonderful husband. But I felt I was missing what other woman had, I began looking at how I wanted him to be, how I wanted him to act, just wanting more, more, and more!

My daughter and I (actually I) felt we needed more. As for me, it was due to a lack of forgiveness, forgiveness I withheld. I did not make a point of watering and caring for my EH at all. I wanted him to care and nurture me!

For a time the Lord warned me about this, yet the more He warned me, the more bitter I became. I came to a point when my soul did not want to hear the voice of my Beloved, Who is so sweet and so gentle toward me.

And so, once again, I was brought to a place of breaking. I had an accident the following year and I spent 6 months bedridden in my parents' house unable to take care of any of my physical needs. In the beginning, my earthly husband treated me very carefully like a fragile queen. Yet his love revolted me— so instead of being grateful— I blamed him for everything. I suffered a lot and everyone told me that it was necessary for me to stop and remain longer with the Lord, in order to hear His voice, but I did not want to.

Then it finally happened. At the end of the same year, soon after I'd recovered and returned back home. My husband left me for an OW. That's when my world collapsed, and I fell into a deep depression. I lost more than 50 lbs. in 40 days. I would faint up to 8 times in a single day. Panicked, my parents took me to the doctor and he advised them that I was close to insanity and might need to be put in a psychiatric facility. At this point, I tore my entire house down, one piece at that time! I did not remember that I had a daughter, I was in such bad shape.

Though I tried to continue going to church, sadly, it was in the hope of seeing my husband. So I began my search elsewhere, everywhere to track him down. Yet this search for my husband only made me more distant from the Lord, for my heart, my treasure wasn't for Him, but for my earthly husband. Even though I knew that when anything takes the place that must be HIS place, in our life, I still relentlessly pursued my EH.

I finally reached the deepest abyss attempting suicide twice, but our God is sovereign and the promises He has on my life could not be changed. At that moment life no longer made sense and I no longer cared about anything. I did not answer the phone. I isolated myself because I did not want to hear anything from anyone. One day a sister who had been a friend since my adolescence, who was also an intercessor in my mother's church, just showed up at my front door refusing to leave. When I finally opened the door, there she stood with a book in her hand. She reached out and put it into my hand. It was the book *How God Can and Will Restore Your Marriage*. I could never have imagined, not in a million years, that one book would overflow with such truths, and would ultimately and completely turn of my life around. My faith, my love for Him, the return of my first love as my BELOVED and trust in God returned within hours of me starting to read this one book!

How did God change your situation Betha as you sought Him wholeheartedly?

I took the RYM book and began to read through it the moment she handed it to me. At first, I was very anxiously, just the name stunned me because I knew it was Him speaking to me. Just reading the first page, I shed buckets of tears that poured down onto the pages. I began to understand why He very lovingly gave me a very unconditional love, and that the Lord allowed me (and my daughter) to pass through this very necessary journey that would change both our lives.

So, once I finished chapter one, I knew I need to confess a deep repentance to the women who sat quietly watching me, who later prayed for me.

The transformation was unbelievable. A change invaded my entire being! Before I wept from sorrow, of recrimination, of hate for being abandoned. Now I was crying with a shame of repentance for so many words spoken to Him, MY Beloved, He who shed His blood for the sake of me even though I was a horrid sinner without deserving His grace because I'd thrown it away and worshipped myself, then my husband after he left me.

I realized that every morning, prior to knowing what was happening, that my daughter and I had passed through the valley of the shadow of death, and even the enemy tried to kill me at my own hands. Even then my HH was there and did not let me be taken from this world by the clutches of the enemy during my despair. Right now I can not hold back tears of gratitude to remember how merciful the Lord is.

During this process, I read the RYM book and His Word all day, every day. As a result, I read the RYM book 29 times. I was reading and writing my journals with such passion. At one time my passion was for my earthly husband, but more and more my passion was for Him and to live every verse of the Bible. It felt like I had never read the Bible before because each thing it said began to make sense, to mean something to me. My heart burned with love for the Lord—as He became my first love, my *HH*. I began to rest under His wings, then every principle that the book advises, God ministered to my heart. Shortly after I was enveloped by the love of the Lord, completely and totally "in love" with Him, and that's when my husband left the OW and went to live in his mother's house. I saw it as a great answer from the Lord where He says to us all: "Seek ye first the kingdom of God, and all other things shall be given unto you"!

What principles, from God's Word (or through our resources), Betha, did the Lord teach you during this trial?

What struck me the most was when I heard about the principle in Isaiah 54. "Make the Lord your *Husband*." This is now how I see Him. He is the most beautiful, the most fragrant, the most loving, the purest truest Love that has loved me in such a way that I feel in every cell of my body. My *Husband* took care of me in such a way that every detail that I needed He gave me. He sustained us both with the best— nothing— nothing at all was missing or lacking for me or my daughter! He was my Supplier for all needs we both had. Ahhhhh how I love HIM!!!!!!

What were the most difficult times that God helped you through Betha?

During the remainder of my journey, at all times, He was there for us. More infirmities plagued us, like an operation my daughter went through. Yet He made it a simple thing, a thing that God allowed us to pass through to use to turn the heart of my husband. My EH began to be reborn anew to us. When he was with OW, he suffered a stroke that almost killed him. When I learned about it, I was immediately distressed, but He spoke to me what I had learned. I had to Let go and that this ailment was part of His plan. I simply went into my room and prayed and asked the Lord to "do His will." That's when He showed me that my EH didn't need me to come running to him, he needed to run to Him again.

Betha, what was the "turning point" of your restoration?

There was no actually turning "point" but instead, it was a slow process that lasted a year and two months after I received my lifeline, my *RYM*, and shortly thereafter he left OW. Maybe this was the point or maybe it was getting the RYM. I'm not sure.

Tell us HOW it happened Betha? Did your husband just walk in the front door? Betha, did you suspect or could you tell you were close to being restored?

During all the time he lived with OW, he saw our daughter and me only once. Even after he moved to his mother's, he spent almost two months not wanting to see our daughter. His mother talked to him every day about it because she'd never learned about winning others without a word. He started to begin wanting to see her when our daughter became ill, it was then that he saw how much I had changed. Rather than always talking, asking questions or confronting him, while he was there visiting our daughter, I was always silent and smiling. Every time he came to our house after that, I did my best. Preparing for his visit by doing as Queen Esther did, how she prayed and fasted beforehand. And each time I always asked the Lord to give me a quiet and meek spirit and favor.

Each time we met, my EH never gave me any sign that our marriage could be restored and many people said no way it would happen. Even though it appeared hopeless, he began to come over three times a week, each time slept in our daughter's room and she slept with me. What I noticed is that when he was here he had such peace. Then one night she asked him to sleep over and not to leave us in the morning. Just 5 days later, I was lying down in our room with her and he came in and asked if it would be okay to lie by my side. We all slept peacefully and woke at dawn. During breakfast, he announced "home" is where he needed to be.

It's been nine months since he returned home to us. We are all new, each of us individually, and also as a family.

Would you recommend any of our resource in particular that helped you Betha?

Yes, I highly recommend all the resources that saved my soul and brought about my restoration. Just yesterday a young wife came to me and I found out she is going through everything I went through. I grabbed her phone and bookmarked _HopeAtLast.com_ for her! Then I went to my room and gave her my _RYM_ book that's well worn. I ordered a new one and told her we will get together when I get the new one, so we can swap books. I hope to encourage her even more to stay the course when we meet. Praised be the name of the Lord!!!

Would you be interested in helping encourage other women Betha?

Very Much

Either way Betha, what kind of encouragement would you like to leave women with, in conclusion?

Everything will work out for good to those who love God.

Do not seek only the restoration of your marriage and your family—seek your own restoration—the restoration of your life with deep intimacy with your HH. And also, savor the restoration of hours you can be reading His Word in order to heal and be transformed.

Beloved, the Word of the Lord is our food, so without it, we cannot live; in it, we will have everything. We are dying of spiritual malnutrition. Even within the church where I grew up, proper nourishment is not given.

God is faithful and He spoke the truth regarding marriages. He said it is His desire to restore your marriage. Yes, His marriage to us first, and this means to surrender to His plan, not yours. He must be at the center of your life and His love is the only love worth having. When we take care of the Lord's things, follow His plan, He promises to take care of ours. Be restored to your First Love, your HH, and then believe that your complete restoration in all areas will arrive—just as He first arrived in my life, in the life of my daughter and in my marriage!

To the One who is worthy to receive all honor, praise, and glory. I love You from the depths of my soul.

Chapter 19

Morrisa

"Strength and dignity are her clothing,
And she smiles at the future."
—Proverbs 31:25

"We're now a Much Closer and Loving Family"

Morrisa, how did your restoration actually begin?

It all started when we moved to our new home about a year ago. I discovered that my husband was cheating on me with a younger woman who is about the age of our eldest daughter and who is also married to the son of our former neighbor. When I found out, we fought a lot. My adult children witnessed these very heated discussions, especially my eldest daughter, who had just had her first baby.

How did God change your situation Morrisa as you sought Him wholeheartedly?

We did not separate, but instead agreed that it would be the best for our family to remain together. We spent the entire next year facing and dealing with various problems as he and the OW continued to meet.

Due to these fairly frequent meetings, the OW became pregnant. She had separated from her husband so my husband became much more involved with her. To keep the rumors and gossip down, she moved to another state, but then my husband traveled to meet her. Even though I didn't know the Word of God as I do now, I still felt His presence. I already felt that I was calmer and did not argue with my husband—even when faced with the cloud of shame I was living under. I chose to simply "accept" the trips he made to meet her knowing that to "try" to stop him would be futile and also destructive to those who were innocent.

What I never expected was that, near the end of her pregnancy, she lost the baby. When my EH heard he rushed off to be with her and comfort her. It was after coming back from that visit to comfort her that he told me he would not meet her again.

About a month later I read a message that he had sent her that made me very sad. He said he loved her very much. At that moment, I just felt that everything was over. It was then that a facebook friend, who I still do not know and who later became my strongest supporter (sending me various verses and later specific lessons), sent me the book *How God Can and Will Restore Your Marriage*. After reading only the first few chapters of the book, my husband commented that he noticed a huge change in me. He said that he had been thinking about breaking away from me entirely but that he had changed his mind due to these changes. This was clearly by Divine Appointment as *HopeAtLast.com* says!

I'm so thankful that due to what I learned here, I didn't try to intervene or confront my husband, making him choose between us or forcing him to let go of her and give me the love "I deserved." Due to this, my EH didn't feel compelled to sneak off but was open about his comings and goings. Thankfully he did not share details, after the text (saying he loved her very much). After that painful experience, he began to share details with the desire to be "open" with me, but I held up my hand, smiled and said, "You don't need to tell me." Then like Erin says, I got up, went over to kiss his cheek and left the room quietly (retreating to a place alone with my *HH* who more than comforted me. This change was due to me starting the *Finding your Abundant Life* that my FB friend recommended. Once I had my *HH* I no longer felt needy or demanding and I stopped hurting, which I never thought could happen until my husband was faithful to me.

What principles, from God's Word (or through our resources), Morrisa, did the Lord teach you during this trial?

What helped me a lot was learning to have a quiet spirit, to win without words. I was never too loud or demanding, that's just not me. Yet, inside I'd be stewing and brooding. Once my spirit was quiet, I was able to "smile at the future." And as Erin says, this attitude in a woman is magnetic not just where husbands are concerned, but also with my children, friends, co-workers and even complete strangers. Everyone noticed I was radiant, which was all due to being in love with Him.

What were the most difficult times that God helped you through Morrisa?

There were so many ways the enemy tried to take us out, to destroy us, and to continue to torment us. Besides the OW, my husband suffered through a very complicated spinal surgery, and this brought about huge financial problems (and surely due to the adulteress we were being reduced to a loaf of bread). Nevertheless, even with all these difficulties, my EH could not get rid of his pull toward the OW or her neediness for him.

Then, a few months ago he told me he needed to go see her, and asked me if I would let him go and stay for a while. It was at that moment I felt that he might not come back because he began being very indecisive in regards to us and our lives. He also said before he left that he felt guilty that she had abandoned her husband for him.

After he left, several members of our family prayed and fasted for three days with me, and my Heavenly Father showed me His strength. I fell more deeply in love with my *HH* during those 3 days and people commented on how much I glowed. To add to my inner makeover, I had changed my hair, lost weight, but most said that there was something really different about me.

Morrisa, what was the "turning point" of your restoration?

Through the days, weeks, then months that my husband was away, he began sending me messages of deep affection, sending them every day without fail. Then one of them said that he could not live far from the family and I knew that God was beginning to turn his heart back to us.

Tell us HOW it happened Morrisa? Did your husband just walk in the front door? Morrisa, did you suspect or could you tell you were close to being restored?

Yes, after five months, from the time my husband had left home, he returned to the honor and glory of the Lord, my God returned to us a new committed man, father, and husband.

During the last few weeks, my husband said he spoke to the OW about her returning to her husband. He said at first she was so angry and called him every name in the book, saying he'd used her horribly. But soon she saw he wanted the best for her and that he didn't really care for her anymore. We sent her the RYM book, and found out last weekend that they had reconciled soon afterward. Two marriages restored!

Would you recommend any of our resource in particular that helped you Morrisa?

Yes, I recommend the books that have changed my life: *How God Can and Will Restore Your Marriage* and *A Wise Woman.* My husband also recommends these books too. He actually ordered the couple's workbooks for the OW and he's ordered *A Wise Man* while he was with the OW. He told me he'd heard about the book from my oldest daughter, saying how much I changed from the woman's book. Truly with GOD nothing is impossible!!

Would you be interested in helping encourage other women Morrisa?

Yes

Either way Morrisa, what kind of encouragement would you like to leave women with, in conclusion?

Everything I read in your books and your online courses was what saved my life. I do not see my life today without My *Heavenly Husband, His Word* and Him, my Lover who guides me today in every area of my life. I feel I'm a much better person, I am a mother who knows how to talk to my children as a wise woman. By His grace and love for me, I am also the wife that God always wanted me to be. The best that's happened through all of this, besides that we're now a much closer and loving family, is that, at last, with Him—I have no need of anything else. My *Heavenly Husband* gives me everything and more!!

Chapter 20

Darcey

"Now faith is confidence in what
we hope for and assurance about
what we do not see."
—Hebrews 11:1

"Pregnant with Triplets!"

Darcey, how did your restoration actually begin?

My husband and I met each other almost 8 years ago, then married four years later. Then, after 15 months of trying, I got pregnant and, surprise I was not pregnant with one baby but 3 babies!! I was having a set of TRIPLETS! Our life immediately turned upside down! To prepare for the births, we sold our small apartment and purchased an emergency home because according to the doctors, I would never have given birth at the full 9 months so we needed to live close to the hospital so we could visit them as they grew.

In an instant, however, everything changed. Just 6 months into the pregnancy, I gave birth to 3 stillborn children.

We were all so happy to be having 3, then experienced 3 times the pain when we lost all 3 children at once.

So this is where our marriages problems started.

How did God change your situation Darcey as you sought Him wholeheartedly?

I've always known God, having come from a Christian family. Even my coming to be born myself was a miracle because my mother had been declared sterile and after 8 years of suffering, God answered her prayers and I was born. Now, she is the mother of 5 children, her last she had at the age of 51 years and her baby is perfectly healthy!! Even though my mother had a husband who was not a Christian (God for him was viewed as "cultural") her faith to one day have children was rewarded.

It was just a year after the birth of our daughter when my husband told me he no longer loved me and that he wanted a divorce. He said he had met someone else and he thought she was "the love of his life." Imagine the feelings that came over me. Me, the mother of his children, who he tells me straight in the eye something like this after all we'd come through!

What principles, from God's Word (or through our resources), Darcey, did the Lord teach you during this trial?

It was just a year after the birth of our daughter when my husband told me he no longer loved me and that he wanted a divorce. He said he had met someone else and he thought she was "the love of his life"" Imagine the feelings that came over me. Me, the mother of his children, who he tells me straight in the eye something like this after all we'd come through!

What were the most difficult times that God helped you through Darcey?

Sadly, when I met my husband, rather than follow what I had seen in my mother and knew personally, I just set aside our King and my relationship with the Lord. I no longer prayed, I simply walked away and thought I could get through life by myself. Even the loss of our 3 children, which had created a gap in my relationship, still had not moved me to change. Even so, God blessed me due only because of His faithfulness, when just 3 months after our loss, I discovered I was pregnant again. Now I have a wonderful little girl.

Darcey, what was the "turning point" of your restoration?

After he told me he didn't love me and about the other woman, I reacted with enormous anger and simply kicked him out of the house, only to find myself at the bottom of a deep pit, looking across a barren desert towards my future. That's when I cried out to God because I wanted to understand why? Why was He having me live through so much pain and tragedy? That's when I heard Him answer me. He said He had to break me because I had forgotten my first Love. He said I had neglected Him and that He is a jealous God. He said above all, He is my King and nothing and no others on this earth can compare.

I reached out to Him, with both hands. I asked forgiveness, began fasting, began praying and continued with deep repentance when He revealed another fault.

Meanwhile, my husband continued to talk about divorce and began to focus on his relationship with the other woman—going so far as to introduce her to his family while we were still married. Also while still married, he went to live with her for nearly 6 months. While at the same time, I kept this truth from His Word hidden deep in my heart. "Now faith is the assurance of things hoped for, the conviction of things not seen." Hebrews 11:1

I did not walk by sight, but only by faith. When it was hard, I clung to the Word of God.

Tell us HOW it happened Darcey? Did your husband just walk in the front door? Darcey, did you suspect or could you tell you were close to being restored?

Then the last week of March, prompted by what I sensed He wanted me to pray, I spoke this prayer to our God, "Lord, I spent Christmas without my husband, I'm through, I declare that I will spend the Easter holidays with my husband and my daughter. Amen."

My sisters, the miracle occurred the next month! My husband called me and left a message saying... "I broke up with the other woman and I want to cancel the divorce— if you still want me. My hope is to come home because my place is with you and our daughter and not in another home. I'm so sorry for everything that happened and also if you have nothing planned, I hope we can spend the Easter holidays together"!! I listened to his message so often, each time more excited. Not because he was coming home, but because I saw the GLORY of GOD and His faithfulness to His bride!!!

My husband has been home for nearly a month, and all three of us are so happy!!

Either way Darcey, what kind of encouragement would you like to leave women with, in conclusion?

During this fight, God showed me so much. I often had visions and He told me that my husband would return, The story is very long, something I could write a book about everything, to tell you all the things He did. For now, I just have to say to each of you. Encourage each of you who are fighting for your marriages. Our Father is faithful!!! if you believe in His Word, you will see its power. But above all, care about Him, never to allow anyone or anything in your life matter. GOD MUST BE NUMBER ONE!

"Now faith is the assurance of things hoped for, the conviction of things not seen." Hebrews 11:1

~ *Darcey in FRANCE*

Chapter 21

Naysa

"The one who guards his mouth
preserves his life; The one who opens wide
his lips comes to ruin."
—Proverbs 13:3

"My Husband was Out Partying with So Many Women"

Naysa, how did your restoration actually begin?

I had been married for 10 years when I discovered my husband was being unfaithful. For years he'd been lying around, doing nothing to help support us, so I lived daily screaming in his face, yelling at him, telling my husband how bad of a husband he was and how I no longer loved him.

What started out as a bad situation got horribly worse. My contentiousness finally destroyed our marriage. My husband left home and left me with my two young children. At first, I thought, Great, now I am free until my husband started having affairs with several women. I'd find out he was out every night partying.

Realizing this had to change, that Bod had to have a better plan for us, I started to change, I changed a lot and decided I wanted my husband to return. But only after a month apart, he was already with a woman he preferred over me and said he did not want to come home. I tried everything or at least so I thought I had, but no matter what he did not want me. I was at a complete loss, until one day while I was looking for a church online to pray, to pray for my family, I found this ministry. An entire ministry devoted to the restoration of hopeless marriages!

At that moment, I knew that God led me to this page HopeAtLast. I quickly filled out the questionnaire and wait a few days just praying I would hear back. And then came the reply! They said, yes, my marriage could be restored, that God loved me, and that if I gave myself to Him wholeheartedly, He, God would restore my marriage. From that moment, I clung to that miracle and the principle in Acts 16:31 NIV, "They replied, 'Believe in the Lord Jesus, and you will be saved—you and your household.'" And also in TLB, "They replied, 'Believe on the Lord Jesus and you will be saved, and your entire household.'"

How did God change your situation Naysa as you sought Him wholeheartedly?

I began to study each of the books I bought on the website, beginning with A Wise Woman because I knew I'd been foolish and had also torn my house down with my own hands. God showed me, in His word, what a bad wife I had been. He showed me how I always blamed my husband for everything that would go wrong. But I realized everything wrong, was wrong with me and so I began my shift from being an ordinary woman to be the bride of my HH. Throughout the day I fed on His Word, I read the Bible, spoke to Him day and night, and concentrated on my children, no longer thinking about my husband. I needed to first learn how to obey God by knowing His Word.

What principles, from God's Word (or through our resources), Naysa, did the Lord teach you during this trial?

The most amazing was "The one who guards his mouth preserves his life; the one who opens wide his lips comes to ruin." Proverbs 13:3. Well, I saw myself reflected in that principle because every time my husband insulted me, I insulted him too. But using His Word to change me, I began to act differently. When my husband insulted me on the phone, I listened without saying a word and no longer defended myself. Instead, I agreed and the insults stopped.

What were the most difficult times that God helped you through Naysa?

The hardest times were when I heard how my husband was out partying with so many women. Each time I had to put him and all my concerns into God's hands. Other difficult times were each time my husband made it a point of telling me he would never return and never wanted to get back with me. But every time, I said nothing, and just saw that the more he said this, the closer we were to restoration. As Erin says, the closer we get the more the enemy wants us to believe otherwise, that it will never happen.

Naysa, what was the "turning point" of your restoration?

Probably when I stopped going to an evangelical church and instead became His church, His bride and at the same time used the abundant life restoration courses to become closer to Him. Almost immediately my husband began visiting the children on weekends and then began staying home to sleep in our bed with me. Although he often seemed upset or angry, repeatedly saying he would not return, I repeatedly always praised my God and told Him I knew that my God was working. And at the appointed time, he would return.

One day as I was having "church" in the middle of the most precious time with just the two of us, I heard God's spirit speak to me and told me my husband would be back in the winter and I believed Him and just began praising the Lord.

Tell us HOW it happened Naysa? Did your husband just walk in the front door?

One weekend, just when it was clear winter had arrived, he came home and told me in the middle of a little argument, "Thank God that I will return home in March or April." Two days later he returned home and never left.

Naysa, did you suspect or could you tell you were close to being restored?

Yes, because when all was lost, when the enemy shouts that all was lost, I'd destroyed my marriage and that my husband would never come back, I know that the blessing was near! That God would restore my marriage and He did.

Would you recommend any of our resource in particular that helped you Naysa?

How God Can and Will Restore Your Marriage and *A Wise Woman.*

Would you be interested in helping encourage other women Naysa?

Yes, I would like it very much!

Either way Naysa, what kind of encouragement would you like to leave women with, in conclusion?

I would encourage you to love and put your trust in God. Believe in His promises because God is not a God who can lie and He is a God who keeps His promises. "Delight yourself in the Lord and HE will give you the desires of your heart." Psalm 37: 4

Dear brides, nothing is impossible for God, seek God, love Him, Adore Him. He wants you to love Him, seek Him first, and once you do, he will return your husbands to you— just as He did with mine. God restored my marriage only because I trusted Him to do it, and He answered because His Word never returns without accomplishing its intent.

Chapter 22

Zinnia

"An excellent wife is the crown
of her husband, but she who shames him
is like rottenness in his bones."
—Proverbs 12:4

"Our Journey with Him Must Never End"

Zinnia, how did your restoration actually begin?

When my husband left home five months ago, we were living a life of turmoil. We did not talk much at all. Neither of us was ever home. He had already hurt me a lot with the things he was doing on the Internet. I told our pastors what he did, and immediately they told me the best solution was for us to have a period of separation.

When our pastors and I confronted him about what he was involved in, he said he felt ashamed. The more the pastors talked to him, the more they asked him questions, the worse things got. That's when my husband said he did not know if he loved me anymore, and the pastors told us we needed to apologize to each other for not making the other one happy. We did that but then right before we were about to leave, and I was glad I'd gone to my pastors, my husband said, that he did not know if he still wanted to be married. He said that this talk had helped him decide to take a break from being married because we were both hurting each other too much. I was devastated, crushed and realized what a mistake I'd made by uncovering my husband's sins. But it was too late.

My husband and I drove home in silence. When we got home, he went in and packed his suitcase and said he'd return for the rest of his things in a few days.

How did God change your situation Zinnia as you sought Him wholeheartedly?

I discovered the RMI site when I decided to fight for my marriage. My heart was broken and, on that day, while I was at work, I saw a post from someone who recommended RMI. It was through the website that God directed me and began to comfort me. I started to read the first few pages and then ordered all the books. After reading several eBooks I then went on to find the courses. I began to identify with the teachings, knowing it's really what I'd been looking for all my life. I was drinking up every principle, obeying every word.

I decided I needed more, so printed the book *How God Can and Will Restore Your Marriage* and I was devouring it day after day as my only meal.

God began gradually molding me, and the tears were cleansing my soul. Joy began invading me from the inside out. Then I spoke with my sister to participate and join me in this journey because she had been having problems in her marriage. With my sister with me, after going through a period of separation in her marriage—she reconciled with her husband. Seeing my sister happy again really encouraged me. At this point, I honestly wanted everyone around me to take the course and so began a group. Women who had all sorts of relationship issues were helped by His truth. We were like thirsty souls drinking up the truth and blossoming!

The *How God Can and Will Restore Your Marriage* book really does explain everything. It proves what I believed I knew but could never explain. God is wonderful and simply obeying everything as the course teaches us—everything—will change you and all your relationships.

God honored me, He showed me how I had an amazing *HH* who loves me and that He is always with me and as long as He is first, everything else in my life would and did fall into place.

What principles, from God's Word (or through our resources), Zinnia, did the Lord teach you during this trial?

With my mind renewed, I began leaving the errors of my way and the more I approached Him and our intimacy grew. He began to whisper in my ear Psalm 37:4 "Delight yourself in the Lord; and He will give you the desires of your heart." Once I lived this verse, this principle and this truth, I could sense how He has always walked with me day after day. My life has been transformed because I have been blessed to live the will of God. I am completely in love with Him, my true Love. I do not know how to live without Him. I am not fully committed, my flesh will sometimes resurface, but with others to encourage, with others to encourage me to want Him above all else, I know that I could never go back to the life I had, living as I once was.

What were the most difficult times that God helped you through Zinnia?

It was probably when I went through financial leanness but that's when I saw how God supplied everything I needed. I'd begun to repeat "He, my *HH* was all I wanted and all I needed" and sure enough, all the things I needed and wanted were added to me just as it says in Matthew 6:33.

When once I cried like crazy, with my heart seeming to bleed, the moment He was mine and I was His God gave me sheer joy, full of laughter. There were no more tears and I was able to focus on my 4-year-old daughter. Through His love that never ended He gave me His warmth and love to drench her and help her thrive. I didn't realize it until then that due to the trouble in our marriage, crises were what she'd only known, times when she'd be basically ignored. My daughter needed as much healing and love as I did.

Zinnia, what was the "turning point" of your restoration?

When I gave up everything to simply focus on my relationship with my *HH*. I was no longer distracted by my restoration or even wanting to get my husband back. It's true that I did not want my restoration any more. At one point when my husband approached me, I asked my HH what to say and then thanked my earthly husband for everything. I said this even though he never cared for us. After he left and even prior to this, I was the one who kept full time employment. Afterwards, my group told me I'd gone too far, and it appeared they were right when for months he did not call and did not try to contact me. Yet I was fully content more than I'd ever been in my life. It was only my HH, my daughter and me. The perfect family.

At that appointed time, my earthly husband sent me a text message asking if I wanted to try again and that he believed in our marriage. He said that this time everything would be different. He was different, I was different, and we owed it to our daughter to be together as a family.

I fainted in my *HH* arms, telling Him I was afraid but soon He gave me the peace, whispering, "It is time, my Love." I knew what God wanted me to do and as He has directed me all along, I took His hand, agreed and our restoration began to happen. "Not my will by Thine be done."

Tell us HOW it happened Zinnia? Did your husband just walk in the front door? Zinnia, did you suspect or could you tell you were close to being restored?

That very afternoon he came home with his suitcases, but he did not bring all the clothes. Each day he'd come back from work, he slowly began returning his things and his heart home. One project our group had decided to do was to make a list of things we wanted when God restored our marriage, and what I couldn't believe is how my husband began to almost check off things on that list. He began to pick things up at the local Target that I needed is when I finally realized what God was doing! I was in awe as I watched without saying a word, seeing for myself that God was changing everything.

The first day he came with his suitcases, he slept at home and stayed all day with us. He did leave, later, but then came back and stayed a full week and then left again. I guess everything really settled down after he'd been home for about four or maybe five months. With our daughter and now with me pregnant, I began to see how each of the teachings I'd learned through RMI and how, by seeking Him first, more than one miracle happened to our family.

Not only was our marriage healed and each of us was made whole, but our daughter was born into a new family where He is at the center.

Would you recommend any of our resource in particular that helped you Zinnia?

Yes, I first recommend reading the book *How God Can and Will Restore Your Marriage* and then find as many women as you know who need help. Form a group to meet weekly and study *A Wise Woman*. Suggest those in crisis to do the *online courses* either alone or as a pair. Then be sure to encourage (by how you live your life and who you talk about) to help each woman find her *HH*, which is vital to you and your group's success.

Would you be interested in helping encourage other women Zinnia?

Yes, very much.

Either way Zinnia, what kind of encouragement would you like to leave women with, in conclusion?

There is so much I can say. I guess the first step is to stop fighting with your husband and stop fighting with God. He has a plan and there is no way your plan will work. God is on our side, He knows everything you need, which begins with the love of a good and faithful Man. God is the One who most longs for our marriage restoration and He knows when you're ready. Trust that God can do all things and that this ministry came from Him as a way of helping you along your journey. I am eternally grateful to everyone here. Thank you, Erin, for your sacrifice. I'm starting a new group, reading *A Wise Woman* book again, and as a group, we began the *Abundant Life Course* because we need to remember our journey with Him must never end.

Chapter 23

Almara

"Wait for the Lord; Be strong and
let your heart take courage;
Yes, wait for the Lord."
—Psalm 27:14

"EH Took Same Courses for Men"

Almara, how did your restoration actually begin?

My journey began around 2 months ago after my husband decided to
leave. One morning he left for work and he just did not come back.
During this period, I heard the same thing from everyone— that I
should not take my husband if he tried to come home, much less attempt
any sort of reconciliation. But I was convinced that this was not what I
wanted and despite the pain that I felt, intense pain at being abandoned,
I tried to find something to give me the strength to believe for a miracle.
That's when I met RMI and my life changed forever!

**How did God change your situation Almara as you sought Him
wholeheartedly?**

Through the lessons I was given after filling out the evaluation, I could
finally see what had cause of our marriage to be destroyed. It wasn't
due to his abandonment but on account of my contentious and selfish
behavior that drove him away. I was very demanding of my husband,
not respecting his limitations and never accepting his opinion on
anything. At that moment I repented and asked Him to change me.

I prayed every day and leaned on the faith He gave me by reading the
testimonies of others who had gone before me and accepting the fact
that I could or should not do anything to try to bring my husband back.
Do nothing except to wait on God. And so, I did.

Each time I'd become weary, or times when I fell, I was supported by the Word and especially in the verse James 1:5 "If any of you lacks wisdom, ask of God, who gives freely to all with great joy."

What principles, from God's Word (or through our resources), Almara, did the Lord teach you during this trial?

The faith dictated in the Bible in numerous passages was the most important principle that I adopted in my journey of restoration. Thank God for RMI who showed me the power of writing down verses and carrying them with me! Along with the verses on faith, the other important thing that He taught me were all the verses telling us as wives that we must be submissive to our husbands out of respect for God. I understood that it was not self-denial, but respect, and I got rid of my pride and arrogance, an attitude which made me superior to my husband since I had more financial resources than he. That had been my reason that he should not have a say and why I didn't believe I needed to accept or abide by his decisions. Through the Word, I came to understand how foolish I was and learned that I should act meekly, with a gentle and quiet spirit.

What were the most difficult times that God helped you through Almara?

The most difficult moments came at night when I felt the deep loneliness, longing for my husband and the moments when I wanted to do something in the flesh to get closer to my restoration. It was in these moments that I realized that the loneliness I felt was in fact lack of faith since when addressing the Lord— there He was, and never once had He left me alone. As I asked Him to feel Him more, I was introduced to the concept of a *HH* and eagerly took the *Finding the Abundant Life Course* and *Living the Abundant Life Course* courses (I'm on Moving Mountains at present).

Once I had my *HH*, He taught me that through faith everything happens. When I thought there were no changes, or I could not succeed on this difficult journey, He'd say, "Almara, just ask Me for wisdom" and almost like a magic spell, minutes later, I would receive an email from my husband, giving me the confidence that I should believe in things I did not see, and never to lean on anything I saw. My faith was growing and today I know that, as Erin says, nothing is impossible with God.

Almara, what was the "turning point" of your restoration?

The turning point was when I decided that I would be putting Him first, making Him my First Love! Focusing on Him and Him alone. I came to the place I read often in many of the RMTs; I began not really wanting my marriage restored. But then, as so many did, surrendering just like my HH surrendered to His Father saying, "Not my will but Yours be done."

Shortly after this, one morning, I felt it important to send an email to my husband (since we did not see or keep in touch) and humbly showed him that I recognized my mistakes, that I understood why he was filing for divorce, and ask him for forgiveness. I also mentioned that if he did not forgive me I would understand, but that he should follow his life seeking God, regardless of our marriage. I was hesitant because I didn't want to get ahead of the Lord, so I asked Him to show me this was His plan. That's when remembered that I had neglected to reply with a gentle answer when he'd written to me about filing for divorce. So, I obeyed and sent it.

Tell us HOW it happened Almara? Did your husband just walk in the front door? Almara, did you suspect, or could you tell you were close to being restored?

Once again, I just have to give RMI my thanks and say—God is wonderful! My marriage, as promised, has been restored. My husband has been at home for 3 months now. And from the moment he came back, he continually says that he loves me and regrets everything that has happened. To my surprise, he acknowledges that despite the sufferings we experienced, it was necessary because we now approach God together! He says we finally we see our behavioral errors and the deviation of the Divine purpose for marriage.

My earthly husband was shocked by how much I'd changed and this I owe to the faithful following of the RMI guidelines and the faith that I gained from the love of my *HH*. I have learned that it is only through meekness that changes do happen; that the contentious woman who once existed was responsible for the ruin of my marriage. I followed the principles of the RMI, which faithfully reproduced the doctrine dictated by the Lord that most of us have been ignorant of and why we have rampant destruction of so many marriages in the church.

I experienced the pain of longing, the pain of abandonment, and even the insecurity of not knowing the principles marriage. But I fought against all this through the faith in knowing Him as His bride and following the carefully laid path along this journey. Learning how to always be praising God, no matter what happened that was devastating and, in the moments when I weakened, I sought wisdom through the Father's teaching. "If any of you lacks wisdom, let him ask of God, that all give freely and do not reprove, and it will be given." (James 1:5)

God is wonderful and fulfills all His promises. Believe, "We do not heed the things which are seen, but the things which are not seen: for the things which are seen are temporal, and the things which are not seen are eternal" (2 Corinthians 4:18). It is true that at times I thought of giving up, believing that things were too slow to happen. Yet because of my love for my HH, I continued on this long journey that at times, seems endless. But, believe me, all of you who are waiting. God knows the right moment and if I had deviated from the principles, trying to get through this journey another way, all the while that He was preparing my restoration, surely the result would be disastrous. Dear bride, have faith and believe. God is never late. He always comes and operates on time even when that time is late.

"Wait. Be strong, and let your heart take courage, all you who hope in the Lord" (Psalm 27:14)

Waiting is necessary, He acts only when we rest in His Word, when we let go of anxiety, and when we have proven we have learned to wait.

The restoration of my marriage came at a time when I realized that I just needed to trust Him, follow His teachings and not deviate from the lessons, letting my husband go, not questioning, or doubting the work that He was preparing. God knows our desires, our needs and hears all our requests, and only asks us to wait with faith, without ever being discouraged.

Even though the trials may appear hopeless and you feel helpless, as if you are alone, do not give up, don't stop believing, do not despair, continue to take His hand and walk along your journey, continue to believe, keep on seeking His face, make Him your *HH*.

Once again, I am very grateful to RMI who taught me everything and brought me so close to God that it made me realize that I did not have to fight for my husband but only to be close to the Lord, being the only One who I really needed, really wanted. Since He forgives everything, hears everything, He does not criticize and the best of all is that I learned that there was nothing I needed to do (fight with the flesh), because it was indeed a spiritual battle and if I have Him as my Protector and my Husband, why waste any energy but in praising Him?

He is wonderful! Do not give up, for right now He is working to fulfill your desires, for He probes your heart and knows what is best for us. Surrender to Him, let your husbands go, for God hates divorce and will bring your loved ones back, and you cannot imagine but your loved ones will come in a "reformed and improved edition," and the best of all this is that your loved ones will be transformed as well. Just in the same amount as you have been transformed, by His love!

I love my *HH* above all things. He changed the course of my life by showing me that I was not a wife, but a bride chosen for Him.

Today I am honored to be submissive to my husband, for I know that this submission is not self-denial, but simply obeying what God has determined that we women should do, be subject to our husbands. That is where my satisfaction lies, for this I rejoice, is the Lord's heart for wives. And I do not care what anyone may say, what anyone might think. I obey my husband and respect him: "Likewise, ye women, be subject unto your own husbands: lest some should not obey the word, because of the manner of their wives, be gained without a word" (1 Peter 3:1).

My husband is aware of this, and my beloved bride, while I was here, thinking that I was suffering in isolation and was fighting my pride and my anxiety, crying and mourning, my husband who was living in his mother's house told me he was doing the same and feeling the same way. As I could never have imagined that my husband who left home saying that he did not love me and that he would never return, he would be suffering due to our separation! I could never have imagined that was happening.

My husband longed for me to look for him, to send him a message, or to create any excuse to ask him to come back. Yet I did nothing of the sort, due to the lessons of RMI that told me not to do it. What happened? My husband, obviously through the work of God, abandoned his pride and shame and sought help to restore our marriage himself! He found the same *HopeAtLast.com*, took the same courses for men and today we are happy and together!! Every day we thank God for not having given up on our marriage, and for having withdrawn from our minds the idea of moving on alone or ever looking for anyone else.

Thank you, my Heavenly Husband!!!! I love You for all Your love, for the work you did on me, and for all the tribulations You presented to me and asked me to go through holding Your hand. Thank You for without the fire there would have been no transformation of me or my husband and I would never have recognized that we, His children, needed You alone!!

Would you recommend any of our resource in particular that helped you Almara?

Yes. I recommend reading the book *A Wise Woman* first and then *How God Can and Will Restore Your Marriage*. I read these books in this order and then reread these books several times and continue reading and re-reading. It became my bedside reading along with my Bible.

Also, the *courses* where both my husband and I agree helped us the most. Learning to journal in talking and hearing Him speak to us.

Would you be interested in helping encourage other women Almara?

Yes

Either way Almara, what kind of encouragement would you like to leave women with, in conclusion?

May you have the faith. Believe that, however difficult it may be, if we faithfully follow God's principles and the teachings of the RMI, your marriages will be restored. Rejoice in the expression "God hates divorce," and give Him the work of restoration, for whatever you ask for in prayer, believe you will obtain.

Chapter 24

Cali

"Let everything that has breath
praise the Lord. Praise the Lord!"
—Psalm 150:6

"Walking in Circles until I Finally Gave Up"

Cali, how did your restoration actually begin?

My journey started almost 6 years ago. My marriage was non-existent, lifeless and horrible. My husband and I let the devil in our marriage. I was a hardcore feminist who thought I was equal to my husband. I was so wrong. The devil and bad friends made me believe that marriage was one-sided. I was very cold towards my husband until he had enough. The communication stopped. We became housemates. I neglected my husband and decided to work like crazy and further my career. My husband tried to work things out, but I was too proud.

I went to so many churches seeking deliverance and solutions to my broken marriage. I thought by acting all nice towards my husband things would get better. It got worse. How worse? It was close to six years of living as housemates. For six years loneliness crept in, bad thoughts took over my life and resentment consumed me. I became overbearing, sneaky and turned into an investigator. I did not seek God at all but ran to friends and family instead. That was my biggest mistake. I spoke terrible things against my earthly husband.

I then went on YouTube to seek solutions and prayers. I then came across the Standers website. I was fixated on testimonies, not Jesus. Then I stumbled into Erin's website and I purchased her book. I was shocked by how much she spoke about marriages and her own personal testimony.

When I came here, filling out my Marriage Evaluation Questionnaire, I said:

Feel like this is the last stop to get help. Married for 6 years. Started ok but found out he had too many female friends. His friends had more priority. Started noticing he was changing, becoming ruder, just did not care if I was in the house or not. He stopped texting and phoning to check on me. I feel miserable. Found out that he is dating a fellow colleague and he buys food for her. Goes to her house to do things with her. Gets home and he will be texting her until midnight. He does not know that I am aware. I told God that I have had enough and that something has to change. I am putting God to the test to see if He hates divorce and if He does that He must do something drastic now because this is hell for me. My husband said he made the biggest mistake by marrying me. He doesn't care if I talk to anyone or if I see someone else. Communication is nonexistent, intimacy never great, I don't support him. I should not ask him where he goes and what he does, it's on a need to know basis, then he will let me know. No children. I ignore him.

I have gone to so many churches seeking help. Been a Christian since I was twelve. But I feel my situation is hopeless. My husband does not communicate he goes out to meet other women. I have tried talking about it, but I got angry, started to hate him and greatly resent him. When I talk it's more of a difficult chore with him. I have asked God why I married the wrong man who makes me miserable and unwanted. I feel like a tenant in our flat and believe I am just someone to help him pay bills. I want help, but my husband doesn't. I'd lost weight. I have prayed for years asking God what to do. I believed, but lost faith. I don't want to be a divorcee.

How did God change your situation Cali as you sought Him wholeheartedly?

I was so tired of going from one church to another seeking help. I was running to man instead of God. I began reading Erin's book *How God Can and Will Restore Your Marriage*. I read her book just once then never studied it until a few months later. When I came across the book again, I decided to put into action what the book said. I was fixed on completing tasks but never sought God to do it. I was so frustrated that I totally gave up my marriage. Things got worse. Then I was fixated on my marriage being restored within a certain time frame.

During this time, I also began submitting praise reports in the midst of everything and it's shows how my life began to change.

"Praise God for RMIEW"

Dear readers, I came across this ministry when I was desperately looking for answers to my broken marriage. I stumbled but I believe it was He who led me here. I read How God Can and Will Restore Your Marriage and I was shocked how I learnt the truth about what I was doing. Everything I have read has taught and convicted me. I have learnt to pray, give praise to my HH, pay my tithe faithfully and cheerfully. My testimonies are so many that it will need a book. Ladies the devil is a destroyer and we should not fall into his trap. Please understand when I first started I did fall and fail but the God we serve is a great God. Erin thank you for listening and obeying Jesus.

"Now I am Strong"

Dear readers, how do I start to praise my Heavenly Husband every day? I was weak, now I am strong. The battle and wars will come our way, but Jesus will fight for us. Sorry for my written English is not great. I urge all women and men to read the lessons carefully and not to rush them. I have repeated most lessons so many times in order to learn and understand. My advice is to seek Jesus every day of our lives. If Jesus has led you here to the ministry, then you are at the right place and time to walk with Him.

"Tithing First to God"

I never used to *tithe* like I do now; I used to say if I pay tithe how I will pay my bills and other expenses. But I was listening to the devil and his lies. When I first came to know about this ministry I was touched and deeply convicted of my ungodly life.

I let the devil play and toss my life around; I can tell you right now I will never make that mistake again. The miracle is that I was in heavy debt but now I am able to pay them off in huge chunks. This happened once I began to tithe. I am able to have peace throughout my life.

My Heavenly Husband now provides for me, my food I never lack, job wise I was really amazed this month.

"Obedient to Tithing"

Praise my HH for teaching me about *tithing*. I will sing the song of *tithing* because of the many miracles in my life. From fantastic job offers to roses since I began to tithe!! Please understand my trials for daily life still come but my HH provides for me without fail. Thank you, Erin, for helping many women like me from the world :)

"My Wonderful Birthday"

Today is my birthday. It has been the best day. Thank you Lord for my iPad air, white roses, a boat ride and a ride on the London eye. I spent the day with my family. My HH is so great. He is my Provider!!

I also want to thank my HH for the last 10 months. I have gone through a lot of emotional roller coasters. Life was hard and unbearable. Then I came to know this ministry. I had anger that was bad. I was a contentious woman. Wow, where should I have ended? Then things changed drastically. It started with paying my tithe to my new storehouse and now my cup is overflowing. I decided to put my HH first. Hence Psalm 150 which is very dear to me...In good and bad days my HH has never changed.

What principles, from God's Word (or through our resources), Cali, did the Lord teach you during this trial?

The lessons taught me that it was not only me going through this trial. Many women just like me had similar marital problems. Coming here taught me to be humble and patient.

What were the most difficult times that God helped you through Cali?

I struggled with waiting for 6 long years. God wanted me to rely on Him more than men. I was expecting a quick restoration, which made it longer. But God taught me to be more patient.

Cali, what was the "turning point" of your restoration?

When I really let go of my marriage. Stopped focusing on my earthly husband. Started seeking my HH Heavenly Husband. That's when I had more peace in my heart.

Tell us HOW it happened Cali? Did your husband just walk in the front door?

My father passed away in February of last year. It was a terrible time for my family. My husband started communicating with me since my father's death. He was caring. I was very skeptical. But I prayed and asked God that He must guide me. It took a long period before it got better. We started to date as a couple and started the communication lines. It was a gradual process. We now chat, laugh and have many first dates.

Cali, did you suspect or could you tell you were close to being restored?

I had no idea. This took 6 years. It was a hard journey, but God was teaching me to be patient. When I tried to fix things on my own, it was like walking around in circles until I finally gave up and surrendered it all to Him. I'd been married for 6 years, then on my RJ for 6 years, but it was all worth it.

Would you recommend any of our resource in particular that helped you Cali?

I highly recommend all of Erin's books *How God Can and Will Restore Your Marriage* also *A Wise Woman*. All of the *By the Word of Their Testimonies*. But the RRR *online courses* are what really helped me focus on my journey with my *HH*.

Do you have favorite Bible verses, Cali, that you would like to pass on to women reading your Testimonies? Promises that He gave you?

Proverbs 12:4
A wife of noble character is her husband's crown, but a disgraceful wife is like decay in his bones.

Proverbs 31:10
A wife of noble character who can find. She is worth more than rubies.

Cali, what kind of encouragement would you like to leave women with, in conclusion?

Never give God a timeframe. He works in His own time. We have to trust a God that even though He may be silent, He is still fighting for us. The devil will always try to get us to second guess God. But remember, He is always faithful to His promises.

We first heard of Cali's restoration when she met our *Living the Abundant Life* brides on their LALTour while they were in London, England.

Chapter 25

Dana

"Wives, submit yourselves to your
own husbands as you do to the Lord.
—Ephesians 5:22"

"Don't Fool Yourself"

Dana, how did your restoration actually begin?

My journey began about 10 months ago when after my husband decided to leave me. He left home for work and then just didn't come back. During the time of his disappearance, I heard from everyone that after what he did (by just leaving without saying anything to me) that I couldn't take my husband back, much less me to attempt any sort of reconciliation. But I was convinced that this was not my wish and despite the pain I felt for what I called abandonment, I tried to find something that gave me strength. That's when I discovered RMI and found HopeAtLast.com.

Soon after I delivered our baby, entirely alone, I suffered from deep depression. The days became very difficult, so I soon went back and became the contentious woman I'd been before. Once again, I spoke without thinking, I thought I was the owner of all truth, superior. But deep inside I was anxious, and I often spoke of getting a divorce. It's when our daughter was 8 months old, I'd gone back to find your website.

Before coming to this realization, I'd sought the help of a psychologist and pastors, but each did nothing to change how I felt or help rid me of my depression. But once I was back, and did just one lesson, I felt at peace again and knew He'd brought me back to where I belonged. It was like a miracle.

How did God change your situation Dana as you sought Him wholeheartedly?

One day on a website I saw a comment from one woman encouraging the other, the Lord touched me at that moment. I sent her email and I contact to ask her to tell me more. I waited anxiously for her to answer, an answer that took days. At this stage, I was crazy, I had lost it completely. But then, suddenly, one day she answered me with so much deep love (even though she didn't know me). She asked me to read chapter one of the book *How God Can and Will Restore Your Marriage*, and so I did, and that's when the beautiful work He began in me started.

I ordered the paperback book and devoured it. I just couldn't get enough. That's when I found HopeAtLast.com and was offered the free lessons.

Through the lessons, I began to see just what had ruined my marriage. The shock was that it did not happen due to my husband's horrible abandonment. But it happened on account of my contentious and selfish behavior, which is what drove him to just up and leave me. I was very demanding of my husband, not respecting his limitations and never accepting his opinion on anything I had a mind to do. Once I learned the truth, I began to ask and beg Him to change me. I prayed every day to be transformed and learned to live by faith, accepting the fact that I could not and should not do anything to try to bring my husband back. To do nothing except to wait on God. And so, I did.

What principles, from God's Word (or through our resources), Dana, did the Lord teach you during this trial?

Faith dictated I had to believe what was written in the Bible as I marked numerous passages and began making 3x5 cards. I focused on the most important principles that I made my own along my journey of restoration. I started with those that were the hardest for me, like how we as wives must be submissive to our husbands to show our respect to God. Some make men their god, their idol, and this is why they submit to their husbands, but this is just as bad, maybe worse than being rebellious. He must be first in our lives pure and simple and being subject must be to please God not our husbands.

For me to submit to my husband meant I had to get rid of my pride and arrogance, which had always made me feel superior to my husband. The concept was shown in my heart when I read the book *How God Can and Will Restore Your Marriage*, but it was the Bible that convicted me that these were His words to me, not just this ministry's options. It was Erin who gave her life up to open my eyes so that the Lord could fill my heart with hope and His healing love. Once I'd discovered that I was doing everything wrong and began to change everything, my entire world changed.

What were the most difficult times that God helped you through Dana?

The most difficult moments came at night, when I felt the loneliness, when I was longing for my husband, and the moments when I wanted to "do" something in the flesh to get closer to my husband. It was in these moments that I realized that the loneliness I felt was in fact lack of the kind of relationship I was missing with my HH. I'd done through courses 1, 2 and 3 and He had just led me to start the *Finding the Abundant Life Course*.

That's when I wasn't just addressing the Lord as my HH, but when He began to BE my true Husband in every sense of the word. He was really there with me and I was really never left alone. When I read when women were still addressing Him as God or Jesus, I knew, to them, He was still far away, up there in heaven. I know, because that's where He'd always been to me. But when I realized He was here, right next to me, when I began singing love songs and not worship songs, my heart began to heal.

Then soon after, when I was just enjoying being His bride, my daughter became very sick, several times it meant I was basically living in hospitals. Yet in those late nights when I was told she could pass away in the night, even though to the nurses and doctors I was alone, I was never alone. I had my Husband there to comfort me and shower me with peace.

Another very difficult time was when my EH called to tell me he was filing for a divorce. But because I was His bride, I was no longer afraid or reluctant. Instead, I had long since let it go. I had a new Man in my life, so I believe it shocked my husband when I almost sounded relieved, maybe even happy. Later I read *Facing Divorce Again* and I was so surprised by how much He'd done what He did in Michele's life in mine, and how this caused my husband not to file. Instead it made him begin trying to get back with me (though I wasn't aware of this until months later).

Dana, what was the "turning point" of your restoration?

The turning point was when I decided to reply to an email that my husband had sent me. It was sort of a follow-up email regarding the divorce. In it, I humbly said that I recognized my mistakes, didn't blame him for wanting a divorce and told him that I had fully let him go months before. I told him I would always be grateful to him for everything, that he was a good man but that I had found true happiness in my life, which was all true. Needless to say, he stopped the divorce and started to reach out to me, treating me better and speaking well of me with everyone. He said later he was sure I'd found someone else.

Tell us HOW it happened Dana? Did your husband just walk in the front door?

My husband is at home. He came back five months ago saying that he loves me and regrets everything that has happened. But, he said that despite the sufferings we experienced, it was necessary because we now have a greater understanding about the things of God and finally we see our mistakes and how neither of us had a clue what the Divine purpose was for marriage or our roles as husband and wife. Today, I am here to simply and humbly thank God—to shout out—He is wonderful! My marriage, as He promised it would be, has been restored.

My earthly husband said he observed my radical changes and I told him I owed these to faithful following of the RMI guidelines but mostly the faith that I now have and my newly found relationship I have with the Lord.

I have learned that it is only through our gentle and quiet spirit, which happens once we truly become His bride, which is what changes us. Thank you, my Heavenly Husband. I love You more every day. I love You for all the work You did in me and am thankful for each and every trial and tribulation You carried me through, making me Your own. I am so thankful I am Your bride.

Dana, did you suspect or could you tell you were close to being restored?

No, I did not suspect anything at all. But when he called me to say he wanted to meet me somewhere, so we could talk, I said, 'Ready or not, Darling, let Your will be done. I only want You, You know that. And yet, I cannot go against Your plan for my life, for my daughter's life and my EH's life either.' At one point I'd thought (actually hoped) the divorce had gone through and that's why he wanted to meet, but I found out he'd dropped it.

Though it was not an "Hallelujah" moment for me, later I realized I can be just as close to my HH as I've been over this past year. Had I known, I wouldn't have been so reluctant to meet knowing it was okay that He was about to restore our marriage.

Would you recommend any of our resource in particular that helped you Dana?

Yes. I recommend reading the workbook *A Wise Woman* first and then going through the *How God Can and Will Restore Your Marriage* as a *course*. I read and reread both these books several times and continue reading and re-reading them. Each has become my bedside reading along with the Bible. But until you go through *Finding the Abundant Life Course* and *Living the Abundant Life courses* I don't believe you can truly be at peace, happy, and glow the way He intends us to be as His brides.

Would you be interested in helping encourage other women Dana?

Yes, I have asked the Lord for this opportunity and I hope He will use me. For now I reply to posted prayer on several websites and send women chapter 1 of *God Can and Will Restore Your Marriage* and also send them to *HopeAtLast.com*.

Either way Dana, what kind of encouragement would you like to leave women with, in conclusion?

Believe in the Lord, in this process, and give yourself fully to Him. Don't fool yourself into thinking He's number 1 when you're still obsessed and focused on your EH. My testimony was as hopeless as they come, and everyone told me there was no good solution. But GOD has proved them wrong. He led me to RMI, He nudged me again using my daughter's serious illness and hospitalization that was necessary for me to take the steps along my Restoration Journey in order to transform me and my life. But not only do I have my family back, but I discovered that I didn't need (and for a long time didn't want) my marriage restored in order to be happy and full of joy.

Whether you want your marriage restored or not. All of us want to be happy. What if you knew that you could be over the moon in love to the point that it erases every wrong you've done and what's been done to you? Would you want that for your life? It is possible. Just let go of it all so you can fully embrace Him.

Chapter 26

Catherine

"The king's heart is like channels
of water in the hand of the Lord;
He turns it wherever He wishes."
—Proverbs 21:1

"My HH gave me a Warmth for the Man I had Married"

Catherine, how did your restoration actually begin?

After I got pregnant I became even more contentious that I had been. I was a woman completely different from God's plan, which I had no idea about at the time. I was a nightmare in the lives of everyone around me that was silly and also dangerous, which led to my coming here. Several times I told my husband to get out, always thinking that his love for me would never allow him to leave me. Until I realized his love for me had died, I had killed it one cruel harsh word at a time.

How did God change your situation Catherine as you sought Him wholeheartedly?

God knew that my husband finally calling it quits would change me and get my attention. Changing me would only happen through my brokenness, as if I was at the mill being ground down, which was very difficult to endure before finding Him. Though it all He guided me the whole time, He never left me or forsook me. He broke me because I fought Him, and then, very soon, I felt His love and I was embarrassed by what kind of women I had been in my marriage. And not just to my husband, but to everyone. I was an entitled diva and I was deeply miserable though I thought this was due to everyone else, never me.

One night, after finding HopeAtLast.com, God promised me later, in a dream to me, that it would completely transform my being and that later, He would turn the heart of the king and the process would completely transform my life.

I'm amazed by how He is faithful to everything He promised and how He patiently taught me to be a new woman. The first drastic change was when I started to be quiet and accept all offense, just to speak to God, giving my tears to Him, when I became totally His.

I became a Zealot of the Lord. Many people called me crazy because the only thing I knew how to do was read the Bible to find constant peace. The presence of God was really all I wanted. Then I found my HH and He became my everything, the sole reason my life, my reason for living. I spent most of the time or all the time with Him, just talking all the time even while washing clothes or vacuuming. Talking to my HH, everyone thought, was crazy. I began to breathe only Him in my life. I got rid of the TV from our living room and everything that I knew would not please God. Only under the calm and protection of His wings did I feel at peace.

During this ordeal, I lost more than forty pounds, due to how I was terribly broken. I was already quite thin. Being broken didn't just happen in my marriage, I had tribulations in all areas of my life. Yet in the midst of it all, I had more peace, love, and so much contentment from my intimacy with my HH. It shocked everyone.

Darling, my Beloved, I want to tell You that these times were the best times of my entire life. I experienced the best that God had to offer. Being able to learn that I could have real intimacy with you, God's Son, you being my HH, me being your bride is the best life has to offer. God, You allowed these trials so I would know my HH wonderful depths, such intimate places and finding the deepest portions of the heart of God where only a few are chosen and only those entering are the broken souls who can see Him face-to-face.

A true honeymoon is the only way I can describe my journey with my HH.

A journey has several levels. Each level will change the trajectory of our lives, but He is in control— so we should not worry when He calls us into the most intense times, times where we learn how to be more intimate with Him. It's only there where we experience being completely in love with the Lord, and it's when God determines that it is time to write the finishing chapter of our marriage restoration.

I hope that my testimony will encourage you to ask Him to take you along a similar journey. A journey where you can be alone with Him, so the love God will pour from your heart. And guard this special time, don't hurry it away, because all too soon your restoration comes and that's when you long for these times, and want to go back to when you only had Him.

What principles, from God's Word (or through our resources), Catherine, did the Lord teach you during this trial?

There are many marriage principles, but what will determine your restoration and what determined mine, was without a doubt discovering and cherishing my intimacy with God's Son, my HH. To fully experience this, I first had to let go. Let go of my restoration, let go of talking about my EH (because that meant he was first in my heart), let go of my church, let go of what others thought about me. Then when I was fully empty, He and His love came and filled me until I was spilling over. He, the Lord, became and will always be my first Love. This is, this was, the gift of my journey. I was taught by my God to love my HH and it's what will be what I forever treasure, my HH is my only, my treasure.

What were the most difficult times that God helped you through Catherine?

Probably each time the enemy used my husband to do bad things and intentionally hurt me. That was until I had enough of His love, and then, I did not have to be afraid. Instead, I wasn't afraid because I knew He was there to always comforted me and each time He helped me to forgive and pay back each offense and wrong with kindness and a blessing.

Catherine, what was the "turning point" of your restoration?

As I've said before, the turning point was no doubt when I loved by my HH, and could really feel His love, becoming His bride. Dear brides, He deserves to be the first in your life, and for you to really fall in love with Him. He has already fallen for you, and yet you continue to cheat on Him just the way I had done for so many years until He broke me.

Once I gave it all away and was free to take both His hands in mine, when I was too weak to fight back. This is when my heart was full of His love and my entire life turned around.

Tell us HOW it happened Catherine? Did your husband just walk in the front door? Catherine, did you suspect or could you tell you were close to being restored?

I realized that something began to be different. For the last two months or my journey, I began to get a horrible feeling that I was close to my restoration, but I only wanted the Lord, my HH. Until one day He told me very quietly that I must open the long-awaited door to this part of my journey, that it was time. A few weeks later my husband called me saying we needed to talk but I really did not want restoration anymore because He had already become my everything, all I wanted and lived for. It's almost funny, because at the beginning of my journey I just wanted my marriage, and in the end, I only wanted Him. He alone was enough and the only One who satisfied me.

When we met my husband opened his heart to me said that he loved me more than he ever had. That I was such an important part of his life. He told me that he had suffered so much while he was gone, giving me a few details, which confirmed many things that the Lord said He was doing at the time. He asked for forgiveness saying he wanted our family back. I could see the sweetness in his tear-filled face, and just at that moment, my HH gave me a warmth for the man I had married.

Soon after our conversation, when I agreed to him coming home, we were traveling to my mother-in-law's house to tell her and his family. A month later, God gave us a new home and restored everything else in our lives. Two months later my husband suggested we renew our vows on the beach with the same pastor who'd officiated our wedding. God is so faithful to His Word to each promise He makes to you during your journey.

Would you recommend any of our resource in particular that helped you Catherine?

Yes, read *How God Can and Will Restore Your Marriage* and the *Wise Woman* book. A woman I never met gave me these both, and today I also give them to many women I know need encouragement and everything else God has for them.

Would you be interested in helping encourage other women Catherine?

Yes, I've also been doing so only my own throughout my Restoration Journey.

Either way Catherine, what kind of encouragement would you like to leave women with, in conclusion?

First, do not give up, stay faithful to your HH and do not be seduce by the enemy who lies. Obey God and His Word. Fall in love with your HH and from there, He will guide you.

Last by not least, enjoy your honeymoon with your HH because you will miss it a lot once you're restored.

Chapter 27

Rhonda

"And do not be conformed to this world,
but be transformed by the renewing of your mind,
so that you may prove what the will of God is,
that which is good and acceptable and perfect."
—Romans 12:2

"Rumor was I was Cheating!"

Rhonda, how did your restoration actually begin?

I had been married for 6 years, but for at least 4 years we did not get along well. We continued living together amidst all of our ups and downs until one day during a discussion we ended up losing all patience with each other. We each were bitterly offended and then I decided to pack up and leave the house. This decision was made at a time of intense anger or I would never have done it, but I ended up doing it because I thought that being away from my husband would make him miss me. It was completely foolish since my husband could not stand me any longer and leaving was exactly what he wanted—for me to get out of his life.

How did God change your situation Rhonda as you sought Him wholeheartedly?

During the first week after leaving our home, I began to realize that what I thought would be a few weeks away from home was much more serious than I had imagined. My husband did not want me to come back. What a shock! That's when I looked for help on the internet searching for restoration and soon found the RMI website. I found the books and read each one as fast as I could. Then after filling out an evaluation and being offered the free courses, I started the lessons and began really learning so much by journaling. Through the teachings of the books, the many encouraging praise reports, I discovered that I was living a spiritual battle, and I began to seek God with all my might!

What principles, from God's Word (or through our resources), Rhonda, did the Lord teach you during this trial?

I made a habit of reading the Bible and talking to God every day. Morning until night. I took a hard and honest look at the contentious woman I had been all my married life (beginning as a teen with my parents) and I began asking for forgiveness from God and from all the people I knew I'd been horrible to. At first, I sought professional help, but it did not get me anywhere, and actually made things much, much worse. As soon as I really understood and accepted that God's will was done, that I'd torn my own house down, and there was a huge purpose for God allowing it (so I could find my HH) I was able to give it all to Him and then HE began to act on my behalf. No longer "standing" or battling for my marriage, I was able to focus all my attention on my new and first Love, my HH.

What were the most difficult times that God helped you through Rhonda?

As time went by, the comments about the life my husband was leading began to emerge. He was very respectful to me, because of his character and the protection of God. And praise God there was no other woman involved in my EH's life. However, he has always been a very lively and good-natured man, with many friends, with many outside activities, and while I was in deep pain he sought to occupy himself by just going out and enjoying life with his friends. I felt very hurt by this. I felt trampled, mistreated, but He used it for good. It pressed me even further, even deeper into the arms of the Lord, my HH, and as He comforted me and took care of me, I felt myself being healed from hurts and wounds from my past.

For a time, my husband and I were just giving us each "time" to be away from our relationship, but a day came when he came to me to say that he had made the decision that our marriage really had no hope, and that it was over. It was a very difficult time, but even so, I could not believe that God wanted it to end. I believed our separation was to give me time to change, time to heal, time to experience His love. So, this again He used for good, I kept my eyes fixed even more on the Lord. I didn't try to change his mind or act any differently. He became all I wanted.

Rhonda, what was the "turning point" of your restoration?

The turning point was when I was already exhausted with so much suffering, and I began to ask God to have His will done, that I trusted and believed that He had the best plans for me, and that whatever that plan was I would accept. I told Him I'd prefer to have Him only, to remain forever drenched in His love. I believe once God knew my heart belonged to my HH, He was free to remove this difficulty from my life. I'd heard it before in so many testimonies, but now I understood.

Tell us HOW it happened Rhonda? Did your husband just walk in the front door? Rhonda, did you suspect or could you tell you were close to being restored?

One day a friend I had in common with my husband came to tell me that she had seen him out with another woman. And when she spoke to him he said he was very well, and when she asked about me, he said he was moving on because I had been cheating on him! She came to warn me to stop "cheating" and to get my life together! I was devastated that this was what he thought, that this rumor, that I was cheating, was being spread, but then I remembered the word that says, "They will have no fear of bad news; their hearts are steadfast, trusting in the LORD. Their hearts are secure, they will have no fear." Psalm 112:7. I meditated on that Word that day and all night, I cried and gave myself into the arms of my Beloved Lord, asking that His will be done in my life.

It had been about 10 days since I had had no contact with my husband and then just 3 days later, he sent me a message saying that he was extremely sad and wanted to see me. That night we met at a local restaurant, and as I walked in, he got up and came towards me. He hugged me and whispered I love you. We sat down, he took my hands and told me he was very sad with everything that was happening, that until then he had never felt the loss much, but that day he missed me a lot and was in complete agony.

He said he'd heard that I had found someone new, that I had changed, and everyone said I was glowing. He said he wanted me to be happy, but he simply could not let me go. He would fight to get me back! Glory to God! God had spoken to my husband, and He turned his heart! We talked a lot that night. I shared Who I had met, Who was making me glow, and even though he was still unsure and not knowing what this really meant, after much talk, he told me to please consider moving back home. I did. That was 3 months ago.

Would you recommend any of our resource in particular that helped you Rhonda?

I recommend the book *How God Can and Will Restore Your Marriage* the book *A Wise Woman* and also taking all of the RMI *online courses*. Without these materials I would not even know where to begin my journey. Be sure to discover your *HH* and *Find your Abundant Life* by taking the course because ultimately this is what made my husband pursue me, just as Erin and so many testimonies say will happen.

Dear Brides, all of us want and desire to have a great life, and the best life ever can be found once you're His bride. Our beloved died and promised all of us this life full of abundance!

"Do not conform to the pattern of this world, but be transformed by the renewing of your mind. Then you will be able to test and approve what God's will is —his good, pleasing and perfect will." Romans 12:2.

To achieve this perfect life, we must renew our minds and let our Beloved transform us through our circumstances and His word. We need to love and trust our Beloved more than ourselves, if we do love Him, we will learn all He wants us to learn, through trials, because it is for our good, He is taking care of us, and of our family when we are with them or not. We have no other option, we are loved enough to let go of our own evil ways, our rebel behavior and start practicing obedience to His word and principles.

Finding the *Find your Abundant Life* is a must-read book. My entire life has improved by learning and applying the principles taught in every chapter. And keep going because *Living your Abundant Life* is even better.

These books demand to be put into practice, just reading and doing nothing will not bring real change for your life. The author shares her own struggles with which we can identify ourselves. In my opinion it does help a lot. Each chapter is something real, tangible and has its own place in our modern life, the struggles we face as women. We can walk side-by-side with our Beloved in our own struggles as Michele does, and she tries to teach us in every chapter of the book.

So, if you do want to read a practical, and real book about being His Brides and a lifestyle change to inspire you to live your own life as HIS Bride, to the point you glow and your earthly husband wants to fight for you, this is the book you must read.

Would you be interested in helping encourage other women Rhonda?

Yes

Either way Rhonda, what kind of encouragement would you like to leave women with, in conclusion?

Dear brides do not give up! No matter what is thrown at you. God said He hates divorce and He does not want any family destroyed. Seek God in everything, find your HH, put Him first in your life, and believe and act like His bride! Do not doubt the love and mercy of God on your behalf. He is perfect and powerful, to Him nothing is impossible! As soon as He knows your first Love is your HH, He will do the most amazing things!

Chapter 28

Morena

"And my God will supply all
your needs according to His riches
in glory in Christ Jesus."
—Philippians 4:19

"Just Smiled But Said Nothing More"

Morena, how did your restoration actually begin?

My entire marriage was a marriage where I'd shed so many tears. Finally, I decided to seek help on the Internet in October two years ago when I found a light at the end of the tunnel! The light would change my history, would save and restore my marriage! My dear friend, I found my Lord that day. I'd sought for marriage help from a friend, but today I understand that it was already the work of my Friend, my dear Comforter, who called me on this journey for the restoration of my marriage, who was preparing me to live an incredible journey with my beloved and dear HH.

During our first 7 years of being married, I was evangelical, yet, I did not know and I had no idea of the God of the Impossible. I had no idea I needed to have an intimacy with God and to have a true encounter with a Heavenly Husband who was pursuing me.

In our 8th year my second child was born, and at the end of the same year, my husband left us. That day my Lord handed me a ticket to pass through the desert. As I was entering the desert, I had with me two children, a teenager who was giving me many headaches and a six-month-old baby who needed constant care. He saw to it that I would not become bored, but would be desperate what my God wanted to teach me. Even though I did not have the knowledge of this ministry when I began my journey, I always believed that God would one day help me.

I wandered for years in the wilderness because the time of God is different from ours, moaning and weeping in fear, despised, humiliated, rejected, shamed, discredited by all especially my close relatives. Until one day exactly 6 years of wandering, such a long period of waiting, when I found the truth, the Ministry of Restoration, RMI!! Every day I was spiritually fed the Word of God, the courses oh my Word!! I was to finally feed myself and my children through the joy I'd found. The day I discovered your site, I ordered the book *How God Can and Will Restore his Marriage* to hold in my hands, devoured the eBook the instant it downloaded. And then God sent an angel to mail me another book! *A Wise Woman*, which was absolutely fundamental for God to surprise me and completely turn in my situation the minute I finished the last chapter!!!

How did God change your situation Morena as you sought Him wholeheartedly?

First God began to transform my heart, had to break me because I was a woman quarrelsome, contentious, arrogant, selfish, woman. So it took God with his infinite mercy to break the vessel and transform me into a meek and quiet spirit. Next, I had to let go of everything that occupied the first place in my life and put my dear HH in the center of my heart and my life.

Dear Brides, it is so natural for us to focus on the things that are around us (whether good or bad things) because this is our nature. But our HH wants us to have His nature and have His perspective in all things. He wants us to know Him and He uses the very things we focus on to bring this purpose to pass because He loves us.

He so wants us to experience Him personally that He uses these very things we deem of importance to bring us to a place where we can experience Him and so believe Him for great things. To us, it brings a level of discomfort, and pain at times, but if we would push through with Him by faith, holding His hand, we will see that this is the only way we can truly experience Him personally and be in a position to believe Him for the impossible!

What principles, from God's Word (or through our resources), Morena, did the Lord teach you during this trial?

The main principles were to first "let go" next to fast from Facebook and all social media, and finally to dedicate myself to reading through the bible— feeding me morning, noon and evening from the Word of

God. My HH became my safe harbor. Next, I devoted myself to the books and courses How can God and will restore his marriage and A wise woman and then Finding the Abundant Life. Without really knowing Him as your HH you are not ready for restoration because it's harder than you imagine.

I recommend and read each of these today and without any plans of ceasing, in order to remain uplifted and in love with Him.

What were the most difficult times that God helped you through Morena?

At the dawn of my journey, I groaned and cried with so much pain, contempt, humiliation, the shame of being discredited and judged by relatives. Endless moments of financial lack, sick children, lack of food, but at these times God surprised me, honored me, did not forsake me and I multiplied the oil and the flour of my jar.

"Weeping may last for a night, but joy comes in the morning." Psalm 30

My journey became much easier and believe it or not enjoyable once finding my HH.

Morena, what was the "turning point" of your restoration?

My husband began to visit frequently, making our house more than just a quick stop. Then he began to stay throughout the weekends. Then as things were going well, a test (or temptation sprang up). My EH had a disagreement with his mother, but he did not say anything at all to me. By this time he had been home for two weeks when his mother called me and said what had happened? I wisely remember God's promises Matthew 19: 6 "What God has joined together, let not man separate" and just smiled but said nothing more.

God was already working, when a few days before the holidays, he told me we need to go get his clothes from his mothers (where he was storing things) and I thanked my HH and realized how God loves to surprise us and to be ready for our final test.

Dear Brides, going through the courses, pouring your heart into each journal at the end of the lesson, will solidify the basic principles to transform you into the princess your Bridegroom longs for you to be. This is not just something beautiful in His eyes, but it is also something to protect and relieve you of your burdens—giving you the wisdom and freedom to live a life in a light manner, as His brides should live. This truth is so needed for us as women, so let the Lord speak to your heart in His gentle way and ask Him to be your Husband.

Tell us HOW it happened Morena? Did your husband just walk in the front door? Morena, did you suspect or could you tell you were close to being restored?

I did not suspect anything at all because my husband always said that it would never happen. I also thought it would take longer, at least a year or two after coming here. And to be honest, I was not in a hurry for him to come back once I found my HH because my journey had become so enjoyable. Yet, He promised that He would restore, in His time, and whether we want it or not.

Would you recommend any of our resource in particular that helped you Morena?

All the materials I recommend. Each resource you offer is well worth reading and rereading and especially to be sure to spread among your friends who are desperate and who have already lost hope.

How God Can and Will Restore Your Marriage was fundamental and in order to restructure my life as a wife *A Wise Woman*. To begin to enjoy your journey, there's no doubt the entire Abundant Life series, beginning with *Finding the Abundant Life Course*.

Dear Brides, the more you follow the plans of the Lord for your life, the more you will bear the fruits of a real relationship with Him. And also you will be able to live in a proper way, free of shame or guilt. You will find peace and the wisdom that will make your life better and will bring the results you always desired. Don't continue to seek restoration for your marriage, leave that to God. Focus on your Beloved HH.

Would you be interested in helping encourage other women Morena?

Yes, I really want to help. Already I look for women to help, sending them to *HopeAtLast.com*.

Either way Morena, what kind of encouragement would you like to leave women with, in conclusion?

God surprises us! That's why you must never give up, never doubt the power of God! He is powerful to change any situation!! What would be impossible for you, for our dear and beloved God and the God of the possible, He is our refuge and fortress very present help in the hour of trouble, with unparalleled love and wants you to put your HH first in your life.

Let your HH become you Friend, Counselor, Prince (of Peace), the Father of your children! I thank my Beloved that I know full well His Love for me. I love You so much, my Darling.

Chapter 29

Alejandra

"Why do you look at the speck
that is in your brother's eye,
but do not notice the log that
is in your own eye?"
—Matthew 7:3

"It All Came to Light and the "Suddenly" Came"

Alejandra, how did your restoration actually begin?

My restoration journey started with my heart! Boy, was I so lost when I thought God had to change my husband and his heart. All together this journey was about me and what my Precious Eternal Husband, my Lord and Savior, wanted to do with me! I found your audiobook in October. I had separated from my husband six months prior and was seeking material to share with a small group of woman we used to pray together with. Months later a pdf of your RYM book was sent to me and I decided to visit the site. Wow! all the testimonies, the principles were so much more real on the website than the copy of the book I received.

As much as I tried to change from being a contentious woman, and a controlling wife I discovered in 12 years of being with my husband my change would not last. I walked on eggshells for a long period but got exhausted from faking it! It took God's presence, His almighty intervention to change me!

I found RMI about a year before I filled out the Marriage Evaluation. When you asked, "Please tell us about your situation and why you have come to us for help" I said:

"I FEEL STUCK! I've been praying, seeking God in my secret place but I don't see anything happening with my husband. I started to serve the Lord at church and to pray for women going through the same, I tithe and give offerings at my church and I keep having this thought that it is not through works but by faith. I have faith but what is really killing my spirit are my 2 boys who every other day ask for their daddy and at given times end up crying for him as he doesn't come to see them. Last time we saw my husband was for my youngest birthday and never heard back from him. All I continue to hear are people telling me they saw my husband with the other person. I'm stuck I'm at the point where I try praying in tongues as I don't know what to pray for anymore. I'm discouraged."

Then when it asked, "What has your husband said is the main issues or problems he has with you and your relationship?" I answered, "I never change. I don't respect him. He is happier with the other person. I don't treat him right. He wants to feel loved."

By then I'd read the book *How God Can and Will Restore Your Marriage* and so I didn't feel my situation was hopeless. I said, As discouraged as I feel there is faith in my heart, I know God will restore because He promised me, He allowed this separation to work on my husbands lack of faith, that He will bring him back as the head of the house with gifts. He will be a father and provider as never before. But my issue is that I want it now. Sorry! I can't help it and its become an obsession.

We have a purpose in God's kingdom, I know it, I sense it. I tried to leave my husband before having kids, after having kids and the love I thought I had got rid of, grew again in my heart. I have been divorced before so this is not new to us. But there is something (I know it's God) keeping us together for a purpose. Like a big one! The bigger the pain the bigger the miracle?

How did God change your situation Alejandra as you sought Him wholeheartedly?

The change came through this principle: "Why do you look at the speck of sawdust in your brother's eye and pay no attention to the plank in your own eye? How can you say to your brother, 'Let me take the speck out of your eye,' when all the time there is a plank in your own eye? You hypocrite, first take the plank out of your own eye, and then you will see clearly to remove the speck from your brother's eye." Matthew 7:3-5

Once I stopped seeing the speck in my husband's eye, God started to work in me! I completely let go of controlling my husband, calling him, looking for him and even the thought of contacting the other victim was a huge NO! I wanted to be right with God and walk the narrow path so that I could get rid of my old self! I hated who I was, I hated how I treated people, I hated how I was not walking in God's design for my life.

Once I surrendered and I stopped checking on my husband's progress or lack of progress, once I started seeking ways to serve the Lord to be part of His bigger picture and take myself away from my foolish tiny drama life— I started to experience peace, joy and a different faith in what He had promised He would do with my marriage and family.

What principles, from God's Word (or through our resources), Alejandra, did the Lord teach you during this trial?

Many principles were learned throughout this journey. the main one is that everything is impossible without Him, the One Who loved me first!

I learned that the crisis did not start in my marriage. It started in my heart and my identity that the enemy tried to steal. Wounds that were not taken to my Lord to heal contaminated the rest of my heart, contaminated my relationship with Him, with my husband, and with my children. But God is wonderful and He makes all things new! I was blessed to be broken and made new! It hurt but I was in the best Hands ever!

Another was tithing to my storehouse.

What were the most difficult times that God helped you through Alejandra?

It was so hard not to see my EH for over 6 months. Seeing the boys cry for him, pray for him and wonder when their prayers would be answered really stretched my faith to the next level. Preaching to our boys when I was lacking the faith, I felt such a hypocrite but then noticed that after they were convinced that nothing is impossible for Him I would fill up again in faith.

Alejandra, what was the "turning point" of your restoration?

Things started to change to the opposite for my EH. Where once everything was in his favor, God changed everything. He lost his clients, closed down his business, got scammed and hit rock bottom.

"For on account of a harlot one is reduced to a loaf of bread" Proverbs 6:26.

Tell us HOW it happened Alejandra? Did your husband just walk in the front door?

It was when my mother-in-law came to visit that it all came to light and the "suddenly" came when my EH said, "I can't believe I didn't see how much wrong I did to my kids." It was a day in July— the day the miracle occurred at 2:30 am. My mother-in-law slept at my house, so after 14 months of not seeing each other for more than a few hours, my husband had come and slept over on our couch. We spent time as a family with my mother-in-law and on the 3rd day of her stay, he changed completely. He knew he had done wrong and could suddenly see. He decided that the next day he would tell the OW that it was over. And he did.

Alejandra, did you suspect or could you tell you were close to being restored?

Noooooooooooooo! Not at all!!!! Even that day I thought it was best for my EH to go back to the US so that the work God had started could be "finished"! I love how God surprised me!!!!!

Would you recommend any of our resource in particular that helped you Alejandra?

YES!!!! This has been a blessing. I followed the principles in *Facing Divorce* of what to do when asked for a divorce, the *courses* 1 and 2 and 3! Each and everyone of them helped me get closer to the Lord as He became the Love of my Life!!!

Do you have favorite Bible verses that you would like to pass on to women reading your Testimony Alejandra? Promises that He gave you?

Zechariah 4:6 NIV "So he said to me, 'This is the word of the Lord to Zerubbabel: 'Not by might nor by power, but by my Spirit,' says the Lord Almighty."

Luke 1:37 ESV "For nothing will be impossible with God."

Would you be interested in helping encourage other women Alejandra?

Yes, I currently am serving!

Either way Alejandra, what kind of encouragement would you like to leave women with, in conclusion?

Hi my name is Alejandra and like you, I was once taking this walk as well trusting the Lord for a big restoration miracle in our marriage. I want you to know that you are not alone! God is with you and will never forsake you! God loves you so much and wants you to remember this every step of this journey He is for you and not against you!

God NEVER fails!!! He did it once HE will do it again for YOU!

Below is one of Alejandra's PRs we posted on our Encourager blog.

Sounds Nuts Right?

I'm so thankful He's helped me to overcome a *Hurdle* Milestone #9. The OW is not the Enemy anymore! I'd like to share HOW my HH helped me let go of my fear to move forward. Also to share a little about how the hurdle I had to overcome and the blessings He has blessed me with since I was able to let go and moved closer to being His bride.

Whenever I would think about the OW my stomach would sink. I would have ugly images in my imagination that bothered me so much they made me upset. So I started to pray to the Love of My Life to please change this. To please give me His eyes on this. Then I understood it was when I learned that... the same way I felt betrayed was the way my Beloved felt when I had my EH first in my life. Everything my stomach sank I would remind myself about my HH precious heart and how I had hurt Him badly by my infidelity to Him. It was through this renewed mentality that God would show me through scripture how the OW would be the instrument for my EH to value what he had at home and had left fooled by the enemy.

And not just that, check this out!!!!

Proverbs 11:8 NIV "The righteous person is rescued from trouble, and it falls on the wicked instead."

Dear Brides, did you know you are so loved that what the enemy intended to destroy you, God is using it to bless you? Sounds nuts right? Well, remember when Joseph was thrown into the jail, which God used to free him from being a slave and placed into his destiny? Yup, same thing with the Other Woman, she is the Victim! She is the instrument the enemy tried to use to destroy your family, yet if you ONLY will Trust Him and walk in HIS narrow path, HE will use it to make your family stronger! Your husband will experience the bitterness of SIN while missing what he had been given. And to make this an even better combo! —your prayers can lead the OW to be a won soul, another bride for our Beloved!

Yeah 2 for 1 deal, the enemy zero. Woop woop!

~Alejandra in Guatemala

Chapter 30

Klara

"Consider it all joy, my brethren, when
you encounter various trials, knowing that
the testing of your faith produces endurance."
—James 1:2-3

"You Don't Know Who You're Dealing With!"

Klara, how did your restoration actually begin?

A complete stranger purchased the book for me after I reached out asking if anyone who would listen from a different restoration website. She sent me a link and said she purchased the book, How God Can and Will Restore Your Marriage which had me floored that a complete stranger would do that. We barely spoke but I followed the what she suggested out of desperation then read through some stuff on your website. Some of the what was said logically made sense and other parts I read were biblical but to me, impossible.

Things like "Won without a word", yeah sounds great but you don't know who you're dealing with. I have to talk about my feelings, all the time and if I do try I'll combust within a couple days. But I read and I read and I prayed and in a short time, God completely changed me!

How did God change your situation Klara as you sought Him wholeheartedly?

My situation changed overnight really or at least that's what it felt like.

When I came here just two months ago, I filled out my evaluation saying:

I've searched and found other Marriage Ministry sites.

I've had some Personal Counseling.

We've gone to Marriage Counseling.

I've spoken to my Pastor/priest.

I've shared my situation with my family.

I've shared my situation with friends/neighbors.

But nothing helped. We were divorced for over a year and though we talked about restoration, each time we got close to making a move, he backed off in fear and I got disappointed all over again. The cycle was hard. What I wanted was to lean on the Holy Spirit and not myself or others. I needed help and found it here. Though when I came I said I am Christian in a church, spoke in tongues and was part of women's ministry—believing in the gifts of the Holy Spirit. I confessed that I didn't know how to navigate this journey He called me on.

What principles, from God's Word (or through our resources), Klara, did the Lord teach you during this trial?

He taught me how to transform my mind. Win the battle in my mind. Keep my thoughts and words to communion with Him only. I quit gossiping and I entered a place where I had complete certainty that God would supply all my needs. I was able to rest mentally and emotionally and knew that God will deliver, even if it was bad, ugly, dark and impossible— that He ordained it and He'd sustain me. Not only did I know I would survive through each and every difficult moment, but He would make me victorious. What else could a girl want!?

What were the most difficult times that God helped you through Klara?

I found this website after my divorce was finalized and I know we wouldn't even have been divorced if I had submitted to my EH to begin with, but I was foolish and very stubborn. This website, or better, His WORD showed me how very, very wrong I was.

I found this website after my divorce was finalized and I know we wouldn't even have been divorced if I had submitted to my EH to begin with, but I was foolish and very stubborn. This website, or better, His WORD showed me how very, very wrong I was. God helped me to keep my mouth closed and endure until He did the impossible.

Klara, what was the "turning point" of your restoration?

The turning point was when my husband turned to me in the car one afternoon, we had been together just running errands and he said, "I really like the way things are going..." I thought to myself, "okay Lord, You are about to do something."

A month before my restoration I found myself surrounded by women who I offer encouragement to. I was excited about my upcoming move (from my mother's house) and I truly believed that this was an opportunity to have a peaceful home with just my Heavenly Husband and 3 children. I was so excited to go on this journey with my HH. I feel like I have the best Husband EVER bc it's Jesus.

Praise God for the Word - it is alive and it does sharpen us. Praise God that He saved me from myself and I don't have to live as the person I once was! Thank you, LORD. My Husband truly is a gift and I am thankful God paired us up. Amen!

Tell us HOW it happened Klara? Did your husband just walk in the front door? Klara, did you suspect or could you tell you were close to being restored?

My husband gently eased back into wanting to spend time together and being there with us. I signed a lease and moved from my mother's house to a condo and he wanted to come with us as well because his lease was up as well. I had an idea that it would happen but trusted God to go ahead and commit to a lease that honestly, I could NOT afford on my own. All I knew was that my Heavenly Husband would supply no matter what.

I could tell, yes, because my gentle and quiet spirit was all my earthly husband really ever wanted. He wanted to feel respected and I was so busy searching for his love that I couldn't do what God required out of me. I was so self-consumed.

I was brought up in church. I gave my life to the Lord at least 50 times between the ages 4 and age 14. However, when I was at a church retreat at 15 yrs old I really dedicated my life to knowing and serving Him. Yet, I fell away throughout my early twenties and came back at 25.

Once I let go of my church, began to tithe to my storehouse, here, and applied to be a partner once I'd been tithing, I just wanted very much to be obedient, make room, and allow for a new life. I didn't realize that I was "religious" until I battled letting go of my church. Coming here

I've learned so much that's new while unlearning many things so embedded in me. I just wanted to keep following His still small voice and nothing else.

Would you recommend any of our resource in particular that helped you Klara?

How God Can and Will Restore Your Marriage and *A Wise Woman* both softened me.

Reading *Psalms and Proverbs* daily kept my mind renewed. And nights I couldn't sleep the *Be Encouraged eVideos* soothed me. Also going through the *online courses*. I could see a bit of myself in each of the *testimonies*.

Do you have favorite Bible verses Klara that you would like to pass on to women reading your Testimonies? Promises that He gave you?

"My fellow believers, when it seems as though you are facing nothing but difficulties, see it as an invaluable opportunity to experience the greatest joy that you can! For you know that when your faith is tested it stirs up power within you to endure all things." James 1:2&3

Oh my Gosh. I learned so much just reading through the scriptures that are in correlation to how we are to be as wives and what our consequences are for being the know-it-all or shaming own husbands. Man, too many times I told people about his shortcomings and faults. I am mortified that I did that. I was upset and hurt that I alone, hurt my husband. I knew it was not the best idea but one, I didn't know how to control myself or my emotions and two, I never thought about what it was doing to him, I only thought about making myself feel better.

Reading His Word changed everything!

Would you be interested in helping encourage other women Klara?

Absolutely. I've shared this site with several women already. Two that I know of have joined so praise God for that! I share with women and people in general things I've learned on this site as well as the revelations I have received while reading the Word. I am hungry and thirsty for more time with my HH and reading the Word. I don't want to leave this place. Ever.

I am thankful to be able to encourage women, friends, married/dating/single to live out the Word. Fall in love with our Creator and Maker and know who He is through reading His Word so each may know His voice. Steer clear of false doctrine and just read your Bible!!

Either way Klara, what kind of encouragement would you like to leave women with, in conclusion?

I would encourage you to read the Word and allow Him to wash you and renew you. It all boils down to a relationship with Him. I argued with Him and took it to Him and went back and forth for a little while but He assured me if I let it go (all the comfort, fellowship, and support from everyone but Him) that He would replace it. I was and still am a little scared or feel as though I am making a mistake because it is so new and uncharted but I know He's got me so, I am falling into His arms. xxx

Would you pray with me? "Lord Jesus, change me. Teach me. Help me to not be contentious and not be a nagging know it all. Show me how to be a good representation of Your love. Rid me of all of the patterns I created in this life and make me new. Brand new. Take all the bad thinking and demonstrations out of my life forever. Replace it with humility, help me honor my husband fully, not just fake words but in my heart too. Teach me to bite my tongue, shut my mouth, keep opinions to myself, watch my words, watch what comes out of my mouth, agree quickly, avoid fighting arguing quarreling and teach me true respect. Amen"

Chapter 31

Shelia

"...so that He might sanctify her,
having cleansed her by the
washing of water with the word..."
—Ephesians 5:26

"Faced Divorce & Delivered"

There aren't words enough to praise God for who He is and what He alone can do! He is the God of the impossible just as all of us have read since finding RMI!!! His love for us is deeper and wider and higher than we could ever imagine and the fact that He loves ME, blesses me. He loves all of us while He asks so little in return—just our love, shown in our obedience, with faith, and repentance, when He shows us what we've done is not according to His word. ALL of this brings healing to our lives!!!

First, I want you to know this is my second marriage. I had been married once before (when I was not a believer) and left that marriage in hate and anger. This time was completely different, because of God's grace and because of where He led me... to you RMI! The first time I wanted to restore my marriage, I found a covenant standers ministry, who told me only my marriage to my first husband was ordained by God. Feeling such condemnation I began doing things I wish I hadn't, which I could share, but it's not encouraging. Let's just say thank GOD He led me here. After reading the *How God Can and Will Restore Your Marriage* book and going through the courses, I knew it was more about me becoming His bride, being washed clean, and if it be God's will to restore my second marriage, He would. If it wasn't His will, what He wanted for me, I knew I'd be more than fine. I'd be perfectly at peace because I had His love.

When my husband was gone, the Lord continually encouraged me and showed me through scriptures and through other things that our marriage would be restored, so of course at first, I was confused (again because I'd read what the standers said). He reminded me that "nothing was impossible with Him" and that if He would soften my husband's heart (as I sought and obeyed and focused on my love with Him as my HH), then this would be the sign it was Him saying He'd washed me clean from my sin.

I'd read in Ephesians 5:25-27, "...Christ loved the church [me as His bride] and gave Himself up for her [me because I'm His bride], so that He might sanctify her, having cleansed her by the washing of water with the Word, that He might present to Himself the bride in all her glory, having no spot or wrinkle or any such thing; but that she would be holy and blameless and whole." All of this was ME, He no longer blamed for the mistakes I made in my past.

The way I found out about RMI was actually when I was at church talking to a divorced woman; she gave me your pamphlet when I shared my hopeless situation with her. She told me so much of what this ministry was about, so I rushed home, and immediately researched your website. I ordered every one of your materials the very next day. And since I also got an eBook, I began reading it right away. Saying it was excellent falls far short of what it meant to have hope again!!

One other thing that made my restoration appear hopeless. Although the Lord had impressed upon me that our marriage would be restored, my husband had already filed for divorce, so when I saw the book *Facing Divorce* I ordered it as well and then found your book *Facing Divorce Again*, which helped me put my HH first above all else.

By reading these books, I responded to divorce without seeking a lawyer, and — praise the Lord—it was your book that the Lord used to convict me of all my sins that I had yet to repent of. Let me say, before coming here I thought I already had a very close walk with the Lord, but I still needed to become His bride, and put HIM first in all things. He spoke daily to my heart and gave me the strength and faith to obey, to become His bride while I simply watched my miracle unfold, and I give Him all the glory along with all my love!

Just about 18 months after finding you, I'm excited to say that my marriage was restored and has been restored for almost two years now. And mine is not the only one either! My neighbors, who were missionaries for over 25 years, now have a restored marriage after the wife read your book through in just one day!

May I say to everyone who's here, it's simply not enough that we take this gift of the truth and meditate it in our own hearts, we need to help rescue women we know. And not just women we know, but women we meet and to be continuously asking the Lord to show us who needs hope today and every day.

So far I have already shared your website with at least ten women this week alone and even after 2 years, I still want to tell the whole world about it! I am always recommending your resources to friends who are in both difficult and even good marriages — I think every woman should do the woman's workbook *A Wise Woman* no matter the state of her marriage! I also purchased copies for our son and daughter-in-law (*A Wise Man* and *A Wise Woman*) and also one for our other daughter who is right now falling in love with a young man she met. I wish every woman could have your workbook before she gets married!

He is the Healer and Restorer and Redeemer and most of all LOVER of our souls. I praise Him day and night. Forever and always I love being His bride!!!

Thank you RMI, thank you Erin, and God bless you and your ministers and ministry always!!!

~ Shelia in Colorado, RESTORED and cleansed!!

Ministry Note: Some of you may be still be struggling by this being Sheila's "second marriage" that God restored. We can assure you that your struggles are probably also based and due to the teachings you've gotten from a "covenant" or "standers" based ministries. You all know what Erin teaches in her books regarding remarrying and adultery—she doesn't encourage it.

However, what supersedes anything and everything is God's WILL not ours! And as Sheila said, she was "washed clean" by becoming His bride "without any spot or wrinkle"!!

Let's remember one thing too, it was the Pharisees who were vocal about the many miracles Jesus performed when it wasn't done precisely according to their "Laws" that were from the Old Testament. They didn't want anyone healed on the Sabbath and when Jesus healed the blind boy they were more concerned "who sinned, his parents or was it him."

"For God did not send the Son into the world to judge the world, but that the world might be saved through Him"—John 3:17

"They [the Pharisees] were saying this, testing Him, so that they might have grounds for accusing Him. But Jesus stooped down and with His finger wrote on the ground. But when they persisted in asking Him, He straightened up, and said to them, 'He who is without sin among you, let him be the first to throw a stone at her [the woman caught in adultery].' Again He stooped down and wrote on the ground"—John 8:6-8

If you struggle with this, please know it simply means you need more of the LORD and HIS LOVE. We'd suggest looking into joining Restoration Fellowship and learn how to become *HIS BRIDE*. :)

Chapter 32

Janine

"And without faith it is impossible
to please Him, for he who comes to God
must believe that He is and that He is
a rewarder of those who seek Him."
—Hebrews 11:6

"He Remarried the OW"

I am so excited to be able to share what God has done for me! My life completely changed the day I emailed your ministry. You may remember me, I was the woman from California who wrote to Erin about restoring her marriage and then my husband remarried. When I first wrote everything was moving forward beautifully, and I was sure that my marriage would soon would be restored. But the next thing I knew, I was hit by finding out (by a close friend) that my husband had remarried the OW "other woman."

When I wrote a second time I was desperate and I asked to find out what I should do now that everything had changed. I believe I wrote in all caps NOW WHAT?!??! Immediately I was sent the lesson "*Husband Remarried.*" I read it as quickly as I could, but then read it three more times before I wrote back, honestly a bit defeated but thanked you. A few days later, I knew that for me to be happy again, I had to learn how to become "content" with what I believed was God's apparent will for my life. God wanted me to give up MY will for HIS will, which was to live at peace and contentment as a "single" woman never to marry anyone else. So even though I was in my early thirties, I knew He would somehow help me. What I had found was something so much much more. I found HIM as my Husband and Heavenly Love! I quickly became *His bride.*

Within only one short year (too short now that it's over), I need to write you again to tell you that my FH "former husband" recently contacted me. He said that he realized that he had made the biggest mistake of his life, which were his exact words!! He had already separated from his new wife and was filing for divorce. So he emailed me and wanted to know if I would consider dating him again. I read something very much like this somewhere on your site, so I wrote back that I would only "consider" any reconciliation after he was legally divorced. But I honestly was torn.

A year ago God asked me to let go of MY will for His, but now He was asking me to let go of the Man who loved me, my HH. I knew I needed to be willing to take God's will for my life again, but this time I was more fearful for I would lose what I had. So when my FH and I spoke, I made sure not to promise my FH any more than I'd consider it, even though he almost begged me to tell him that I'd marry him again!

My struggle may have been partly due to me sharing this principle of COMPLETELY letting a husband go with several other women whose husbands had remarried like mine had. I guess I just didn't think for a second my heavenly honeymoon would be over so soon.

Of course I relented in my heart to accept His will for my life and about four months later my husband was free of the OW (no longer married) and contacted me again. He began by explaining that once I left him alone (and let go), he was able to feel the pain of the mistake he made and his horrible decision to marry the other woman (that he said he knew even before he married her). He told me when I kept chasing him, calling him and following his every move on FaceBook (before I closed my account) he thought marrying her would get me to leave him alone. What he didn't know was that it wasn't him getting married, but it was me denouncing my following the standers creed and finding my HH.

No matter how it really happened, once he stopped seeing me on FB or hearing from me (calling, texting and sending him cards) he began thinking about me again. So that's when he began to track me down. And after finding me, even though he hadn't planned to get divorced, because I wasn't excited to hear from him like he thought I'd be, that's when he realized what he'd lost. We had put off having children (my decision before I read the chapter in *A Wise Woman*) so not only did he propose to me that night, he also asked if I'd be willing to have children with him and I said Yes. (The OW had promised that she and he would have kids, but I confess I did pray her womb would be closed before I fully let go when I read the *RYM* book).

Dear friend, for any of you who are afraid to let go, I mean really let go, please walk away from what you're holding on so tightly to and trust God. It's fear that's making you hold onto what God wants you to let go of. You need to be willing to want HIS will over your own, whether that's to let go and live as His bride or if it's to accept that His will to live as the wife of an EH or FH like He asked me.

So far we haven't gotten pregnant, but I am confident in His will. I've even been pushed to pursue IVF treatments, but like everything in my life, nothing is impossible for God. If He wants to bless us with a baby, He will. And one more thing, I didn't stop being His bride and He is even more my HH. If anything, I need Him more now than before. It's just harder to find the time to have Him all to myself, but that makes our time together even more special!

The last thing that I need to confess is that I am always confused and just a bit hurt when I meet women who have a slightly different situation than mine, and they're unable to find a restored marriage similar to theirs (in any of the hundreds of testimonies that you have in your books or on your site) so they begin to ask me to show them one exactly like theirs. If it's not exactly like theirs, they have absolutely no faith to trust Him! "And without faith it is impossible to please Him, for he who comes to God must believe that He is and that He is a rewarder of those who seek Him," (Hebrews 11:6). "Sighing deeply in His spirit, Jesus *said, "Why does this generation seek for a sign? Truly I say to you, no sign will be given to this generation." (Mark 8:12). When Erin was trusting God for her restoration, I read that she had NO ONE, not ONE other restored marriage she'd ever heard about. None of the pastors she spoke to gave her any hope, and no ONE gave her any encouragement either. And because it was over 25 years ago, I don't think there was a way to Google for a site or books or anything else either. It was through the faith of just one woman that we've all been encouraged to find not just restored marriages but HIM!

So sorry this is so long but I just had to share everything He's done with you and hope it helps someone else who has no hope.

~ Janine in California, RESTORED

*UPDATE: Janine and her husband were blessed to welcome a son two years after they were remarried after reading the book *Supernatural Childbirth.* Janine conceived naturally and had a supernatural birth we hope to hear details about and share it with you soon!

Chapter 33

Yvette

"All the paths of the Lord are
mercy and truth, to such as keep
His covenant and His testimonies."
—Psalm 25:10

"Restoration! God has Changed my Life!"

In October, the worst possible thing I could imagine happened. My husband of 12 years told me that he wanted to leave. I was devastated, and didn't know what to do. Desperately, I began searching and praying for something to show me what I needed to do to gain back the man I loved. I found Restore Ministries over the Internet a few weeks later. I know it was the Lord who led me to the website. I immediately ordered the Restore Your Marriage and A Wise Woman. What a blessing! I read and read until I couldn't read any more. God started showing me all that I had done to cause my husband to leave our home. I was contentious, spiritually prideful, and arrogant. God convicted me of my sins, and I pleaded with Him to help me change. Praise God, He had mercy on me and changed my life!

As I continued to pray and fast, I noticed my husband's heart softening towards me a few months later. He began spending more time at our home and staying for longer periods of time. Around Christmas Time, the Lord worked a miracle. He led my husband to spend the night so that our children would not have to be without him on Christmas Day! Praise the Lord! After that, and into the New Year, he started to spend less time with the OW and more with the children and me. We started to communicate as husband and wife again, and a month later, he decided to give our marriage another chance. He said that he did not want to see 12 years of marriage wasted away, and realized his life was turning upside down without us!

On February, my husband moved back home! We are learning to seek the Lord first in everything we do. As I look back, I realize that the Lord was not my first love. My husband was. I learned that I had to release my husband and my marriage to God in order to see any kind of turnaround. When I did, it worked! God is so very gracious, awesome and loving. I thank Him for allowing me another chance to be the wife I was called to be. I pray that each day brings about further blessings from the Lord and that I never lose sight of Him again. My desire is to serve Him day and night for the rest of my life.

I also want to thank Restore Ministries and my prayer partner for not giving up on me. You encouraged me, supported me, and rebuked me. You helped me to not be fearful and to continue to believe that my husband would one day return. God bless you, Erin, for your ministry! May the Lord continue to keep you in His tender care.

~Yvette, RESTORED in Pennsylvania

Chapter 34

Daisy

"Then Jesus said, "Did I not
tell you that if you believe,
you will see the glory of God?"
—John 11:40

"Jesus Raised Her Marriage from the Dead!"

Praise the Lord, in order for the Lord to get my attention, He removed my husband from me two and a half years ago. My old life and marriage had to be destroyed for God to begin something new in my life and marriage.

I was a "Christian girl" all my life—a Pentecostal going to church on Sundays and tearing down my household as a foolish woman on other days. When my husband left in July after our tenth anniversary, he told me he would never come back and he headed straight to his lawyer friends, who all decided that it was in his best interest to divorce me and start new life without me and our daughter, who was nine years old at that time.

At this point I knew he was serious and he was leaving. I was so desperate that I turned to my senior pastor for help. He and his wife just hugged me and that was it. I turned to all my church friends, but all they said was to forget about him.

From the beginning, when my husband left, God put in my heart that He would restore my marriage but I didn't know how. The Lord gave me John 11: Jesus raises Lazarus from the dead.

I knew He allowed my situation of separation and divorce for His glory. I went crazy and went to different bookstores, including Christian bookstores, but I couldn't find anything about restoring marriage. Then I starting going on Internet looking at different Christian sites about marriage. One night I was crying so hard as I was typing. It was the divine power of the mighty Abba Papa Almighty, my very being, my all and all—oh, I love Him and cannot praise Him enough! Hold my hand and type "restore marriage" and push the button "search." Praise the Lord—there it was!—the RMI website looking me right in the face! I screamed so loud and call my daughter to come and see what mama has found. We both were so excited—I knew God was behind all this.

The next day I called RMI and said, "I want to become a member," and I signed up right away. I ordered the How God Can and Will Restore Your Marriage book and other materials because I was so desperate, hoping against hope, and I was willing do whatever God wanted me to do! I didn't have the money but I charged it on a credit card—I would rather be buying something to do with the kingdom of God and in debt than spending on my worldly desires and debt.

As I sought the Lord, He drew near to me, and at the same time He removed people I was depending on and took them away from me. He changed me and taught me to depend on Him by running to Him when in need instead of to the arm of flesh.

He taught me to really pray—I mean pray like I never did before—and to fast. One of the biggest things He broke me of was never to talk about my situation to anyone but Him and Him alone. As I obeyed Him on that, He was so faithful to me that most of my close friends at work didn't even know that my husband had been gone.

God has protected me and our little girl. He made me into a lover of His Word, and now I seek Him in everything I do in my life. Jesus has become not just my Savior but also my precious Lord and best friend, the Lover of my very soul and being. Glory to His powerful name: Jesus!

As I sought the Lord and became so close to Him, my situation didn't get better but worse. My husband went ahead and divorced me, even though the hate wall was down. I didn't hire any lawyer; I didn't have to because I have the best lawyer on my side—His name is Jesus.

God told me two months in advance as I was walking my dog in the park that the divorce would go through in order for my husband to heal. God said He would allow it, but "don't be afraid—I am with you." At that time I had the peace that passes all human understanding in my soul. But that didn't stop me from fasting and praying against that divorce going through. After the divorce, things turned around for good.

God taught me during this trial so much, including that God is faithful to His Word, and He is merciful and full of love. The resources from RMI—God used them to teach me, including the How God Can and Will Restore Your Marriage book, the Wise Woman workbook, and the *Be Encouraged tapes and videos.* I very much recommend them to everyone—they were a big part of my desire to restore my marriage. I knew that what God could do for you, sweet sister Erin, He could do for me too.

The two and a half years was difficult not just for me but for our little girl also. Finding out about the OW was hard—I felt helpless because I wasn't anything, I wasn't his wife legally, and I cried into the arm of God. My daughter was very sick because I could not afford groceries—I bought the cheapest frozen pizza, and she got sick from eating it. I had dropped her off to her daddy's place before I went work. He called me later and asked me what I fed her the night before. I answered "pizza." He asked where I got it, and I told him, and he got mad. I didn't say anything back to him—I just took all the insults and told him I would do better next time.

I went right into my Father's mighty arm and cried, emptying everything to Him. I said, "Father, he was with the OW eating dinner in the expensive place in town, buying good food, whole food, and taking expensive trips, and here I am doing the best I can to put food on the table for my precious baby girl and yet it is not good enough. Lord, I am the wife of his youth. I helped him through his college and even helped him through finishing his doctor's degree. But now to him I am nothing." I told God I don't care about any person or any thing anymore—all I want is just Him and me. And He held me and told me that "soon the wicked will be cut off and destroyed and you will go in and conquer the land." As He whispered this sweet promise into my ear four months ago, I fell asleep into His arms.

The turning point in our restoration was when I let God be God and just loved Him and asked Him to give me the grace to love my new husband with His unconditional love. God brought him to a point where nothing was working for him. He was so miserable with the OW, at his work, because my God built a wall around him and he could not find his lovers and could not overtake them. Then he said, "I will go back to my wife for it was better for me."

Those were his words, which he told me around June, when he invited me and our daughter to our summer cabin. He told me he had ended the relationship with the OW, and told her he has had a girlfriend all along, that she is his best friend and soul mate and he loves her and wants to be with her. I turned to him. "Who is that girl?" I asked. He turned to me with pure love in his eyes and said, "This girl is you." He told me, "You're the best. I don't know what else I was looking for." I was praising the Lord in my spirit as he was saying these things!

On Wednesday at 2:00 or 3:00 in the morning, the Lord woke me up to pray. I asked the Lord, "Pray for what and for who?" One of the lesson the Lord taught me during this trial was that He would wake me up in the middle of the night to pray for a certain person or situation. The Lord knew the typical questions I would ask: "Lord, now what, who, and why? Do I have pray, or can it wait until I am fully awake?" God always wins out.

Anyway, on that night He said, "Pray for your husband's deliverance." I said, "From what?" He said, "From the enemy." So I began praying half asleep, then the Lord said, "Stop praying and just keeping praising Me and thanking Me, for I have delivered him from the land of the enemy and I will bring him home to live in peace and safety."

Around 7:00 a.m., I got ready and got the house clean and I was so excited. And when I asked my daughter to get ready, she looked me and said, "Mom, you okay?" I said, "Yes I am." I told her that God woke me up and said He is bringing daddy home today—daddy has been delivered from the land of the enemy!

Around 9:00 a.m., my new husband called. When our daughter answered the phone, he said, "I need to talk to Mom." I said hi, and he said, "I really need you. Would you come and take me home?" He was calling from his apartment. When I put down the phone, I began praising God with my daughter and our dog, jumping and shouting.

After that, I drove to his apartment and brought him home. He called his landlord to terminate his lease, even though he has to pay for an extra month. He called his family and told them about us. I know God brought him home—I had nothing to do with it. God did all the changes in me, and He will continue to change me more into His image every day. Glory and honor to His holy name!! I bless Him! Thank You, Jesus, for your sacrifice—one more marriage has been restored!

~Daisy, RESTORED in Wisconsin

Chapter 35

Lisa

"Be still, and know that I am God…"
—Psalm 46:10

"Restored through Humility!"

Five years ago, my husband and I got married. A few months after that, I found out that he had someone else, and he told me that he felt it best to get a divorce. I was devastated and, needless to say, depressed. This went on for almost two and a half years. During those years, I continued to go to church and read Scripture, mostly the Psalms and Proverbs.

During that time, God took me to the wilderness to where only He and I spent time together. Only through total brokenness did God really begin to speak to me. I had so many bad habits that involved control and anger. He had to get rid of those before He could really work in my marriage. I kept reading about the restored marriages and wondered why mine was not happening. Now I realize that through brokenness, prayer, and fasting God breaks through to us. He was there all of the time, yet with my tainted view of life, I never really saw what He was doing.

I found Restore Ministries through a woman at our church who led me to Erin. Erin prayed with me and gave me a Restore Your Marriage book that was originally intended for someone else—the Lord knew I needed it desperately! I also recommend the A Wise Woman. The Scriptures were especially helpful.

God began to change me and soften my heart. He taught me humbleness (something I have never been very good at) and He taught me to look to Him and not at my circumstances. He taught me to run to His Word and not my friends. Better yet, He taught me to pray instead of speaking my mind immediately! During this past two and a half years that my husband has been back home, our relationship improves every day. I see God working on my husband's heart in areas that I have been praying about for a long time. He continues to work on my heart because the enemy loves to creep in and steal my joy if he can.

God's Word kept telling me to "wait." I hated that word at one time. I even told the Lord that I didn't like waiting. His loving patience kept me waiting. Waiting on Him, waiting until my heart was ready for what He had in store for me, waiting for the Lord to work on my husband's heart. "Be still and know that I am God"—that was something that God really had to teach me. I am a person of action and wanting to fix things, right now! God's Word (especially the Psalms) helped me to realize that waiting on God is the only way to have victory in any circumstance.

I can remember when the OW would call the house or my husband would leave to go call her. I would begin praising the Lord and telling Him how much I loved Him. When I didn't know what to say, I would repeat over and over, "By Your grace, Lord, cover me in Your grace..."

Oftentimes, my husband would come in more loving or would want to spend time with me. Also, it often turned out that he wasn't doing what I feared the most. I truly believe that by praising the Lord during those times, the enemy was sent back to where he belongs. Prayer and praise break the bonds of the enemy!!

I would say that the turning point of my marriage restoration was when I took my eyes off of my marriage and put them on the Lord. Things didn't happen overnight for me. It has been a slow process, but I think that I know why: God knows my temperament, my strong will, and my control issues. I believe that God brings my marriage along at a pace that He knows is best for me and my husband. I continually pray for His wisdom, His guidance, His eyes to see with, and a heart like Jesus'. He continues to show me how He is restoring our marriage one day at a time.

I praise the Lord because He loves me enough to teach me His ways as I seek His guidance. My husband wants to be with me, He wants to go to church with me, and He gets more and more involved with time. He speaks of us growing old together and makes plans for our lives in the future. He is becoming more sensitive to my needs and wants. He also communicates to me in a way that helps ease any insecurity that may linger from what happened in the past.

God has truly been transforming both of us, which is my prayer. I see God working in our lives in ways that only the Lord knows how! He is such a faithful God Who really loves us and knows us!

~Lisa, RESTORED in Missouri

Chapter 36

Michelle

"It is a trustworthy statement, deserving
full acceptance, that Christ Jesus came into
the world to save sinners, among whom
I am foremost of all."
—1 Timothy 1:15

"Restored! And He Alone is the Pearl of Great Price!!"

Praise the Lord! He has glorified Himself through the work He has done in our marriage—and in me! I thank Him for the testimony He has given me and pray that He would receive all the glory for what is written here.

First, I must say that I do not deserve anything that He has done! The reason my marriage was such a mess to begin with was because of my own sin and selfishness. This marriage is my second one. My first marriage ended in divorce after I was in adultery. After my divorce, I am ashamed to say, I continued to live a lifestyle that was desperately wicked. Even though I had two young daughters, I made parties, men, and drinking my life, and I encouraged other women in the same lifestyle! Worse, I used abortion as birth control. (Even an unbeliever would be horrified to hear how many abortions I had, which goes to show that even those who call themselves "pro-choice" know deep down that abortion is an abomination to God.)

I became heavily involved in New Age and Eastern spirituality and truly believed I could control my own future. Sadly, at the time, I thought I was happy, in control, at peace, and the life of the party. (It never occurred to me to wonder whether "peacefulness" could really coexist with "life of the party.") Now I realize how spiritually dead I really was!

When I met the man who would become my second husband, we didn't date long before we became intimate. Not only did I become pregnant, but I deceptively chose to become pregnant because I wanted another child! (Why this time and not the others? I really must have thought I was playing god!) I did not expect him to marry me and selfishly made every decision for my own purposes. I also lied to him and did not tell him of my deception. He graciously asked me to marry him, though, because of his love for his son, his desire to make an honorable decision, and his love for me (which, however imperfect, was certainly more mature than my love for him!).

We were married by three people: a Greek Orthodox monk in full regalia, a New Age priestess (for lack of a better term), and a female pastor of a very liberal church (that proclaimed not salvation through Jesus Christ alone but "tolerance and social justice"). During our wedding ceremony, we promised to love and adore each other, but only after we first loved ourselves!! No traditional vows for us!

The fruit was evident immediately: At our wedding reception, we ended up in a huge argument, and I selfishly walked out of my own reception, dragging my friends with me. Praise God—He used one of them to tell me point-blank that my self-centered New Age beliefs and the sinful life I was living without God were the reasons things had gotten so bad! A few days later, I prayed to God to save me from my own sin. I wasn't sure He was real, but I asked Him to show me and save me if He was.

As a child, I had "accepted Christ" many times, but in retrospect I see that what was so obviously missing was an understanding of my sin! Back then, I was a "good girl"—I didn't see any sin anywhere. Ironically, I had often listened to testimonies in church from people whom God had delivered from terrible sins—drugs, alcohol, prostitution, etc.—and I remember thinking that I wanted a testimony like that and how sad it was that "I would never have one." God in all His wisdom (and certainly not without a sense of humor) must have taken that as a prayer, because I now have that kind of testimony—one that glorifies Him and Him alone!

After I prayed and asked God to save me, He definitely showed me He was real. I had asked specific questions of Him in my prayer that day, and within a week He had answered all of them! I knew beyond a shadow of a doubt that He was real, and that the shed blood of Jesus Christ had saved me from all of my sins!

He began to show Himself to me on our honeymoon. My husband and I went to a beach house in South Carolina, where we fought constantly. (Can you imagine what my husband thought? That I had "planned" all along to "change all the rules" as soon as we were married!) But our time away became my honeymoon with Jesus, and He began to transform me as I read His Word every day.

He also showed me that it was His timing when He called me to Himself, and the fact that it was after our wedding (had it been a week before, we probably wouldn't have married!) meant that I was to remain married, that God had a plan and a purpose for this marriage. When things got bad later and people told me we were unequally yoked, I could honestly tell them that we were very equally yoked when we married, and it was clearly His will that we remain together.

When we got back from our honeymoon, the Lord convicted me that I needed to tell my husband the truth about our son, that I had become pregnant on purpose. It was one of the hardest things I have ever had to do, but I knew that I had to be obedient and leave the results in God's hand. Unfortunately, after I confessed, things got worse, not better. I never doubted that I had done the right thing by telling him, yet admitting my willful deception seemed to be the beginning of a root of bitterness and distrust in my husband's heart that only grew worse (and I certainly couldn't blame him!). I see now that I was probably the most contentious woman who ever lived—we were invariably arguing about something, no doubt because I was constantly criticizing him!

On top of that, I was like the adulterous woman—my feet were never home. One weekend, after being away on business, I returned home and felt something was amiss. I noticed a woman's hair on our couch (bright red—not my color!) and immediately accused my husband of having someone over. He admitted that a woman had been in our house but said that it was innocent. (The children had been with him, and in retrospect I am sure he was speaking the truth. I obviously didn't know or take to heart the fact that "love believes all things.") Immediately I kicked him out of the house to make a point that I would not be treated "that way," then I proceeded to shame him by telling everyone I knew what he had "done."

There had also been physical altercations, which I first provoked and then used to get sympathy from anyone who would listen. There was also a lot of drinking, but instead of "love covering all transgressions" (Prov. 10:12, 1 Pet. 4:8), I slandered my husband by talking loudly about that too! Of course my friends and even people in the church told me to practice "tough love," to take a stand against being "treated that way," and said that my husband would "never change" if I continued to "enable" him. I don't repeat this to slander my husband now but instead to show you that God wants to glorify Himself even in situations like these that seem impossible—but I didn't give God a chance! He certainly didn't need to defend someone who was already busy defending herself, or to be righteousness for one who was so self-righteous! By listening to the world (wanting to have my "ears tickled"), I continued to justify my own sinful behavior.

What a Pharisee I was! I told others of my husband's sins but could not see my own contentiousness, jealousy, self-righteousness, and insubordination (1 Sam 15:23). God showed me later that my "tough love" stance was actually manipulation!

He also later showed me that I was responsible for the times my husband had become physical ("a fool's mouth calls for blows," Prov. 18:6). In fact, I had provoked it every time! Once I learned to control my tongue, God took care of the rest. God had shown me earlier through Scripture that if my husband were truly a threat, He could remove him immediately. But obviously He didn't because it wasn't my husband who was so bad but me!!

I also learned later that the times when he has a few drinks are times that God has chosen for me to be away from my husband (He removes "lover and friend far from me," Ps. 88:18) in order to have me all to Himself—I am to be in the Word during those times, praying and rejoicing for my time alone with Him!

After about two months of my husband's being out of the house, I felt led by the Lord to fast, something I had never done before. By the middle of the second day, I knew beyond a doubt that I was to ask my husband to return home—and that I never should have asked him to leave in the first place.

Things got better for a time, but again I fell into the trap of distrusting, snooping, and following up on everything my husband said or did—and it became almost an obsession. We tried counseling on several occasions, which came to nothing and in fact often made things worse. I did have a single moment of truth with one counselor, who told me, "You may not be able to trust your husband, but you can trust God." That convicted me for a short period of time, but then (with the counselor's blessing!) I was back trying my own hand at controlling the situation.

My distrust came to a head a few years later, when I ended up asking God to show me whether my husband was or had been in adultery (I obviously forgot to pray about the future!). I promised to let go and trust Him if the answer He gave me was "no"—and it was! Immediately God enabled me to stop all of my snooping, and I began for the first time to really live by faith. The verse "For your Maker is your Husband" (Isa. 54:5) became real to me—it was (and still is!) one of my favorite verses in the Bible.

For the next six months, things got better. My faith continued to grow, and my relationship with the Lord was becoming more intimate. I was trusting Him in a new way. And then one night, I was prompted to pray in a way I never had before, for any hidden things to come to light. I was thinking in my mind of pornography or something similar, having no idea what God actually had in store. My last prayer before falling asleep that night (prayed with a real sense of not necessarily trepidation but expectancy that something was about to happen) was that God would "bring all things done in darkness to light."

The next morning at 4:00 a.m., while it was still dark outside, I was awakened by first our home phone, then my cell phone, and then my office phone ringing. I didn't know it until I checked messages later that morning, but God had answered my prayer before the sun even rose! It was the husband of the OW, calling to tell me that my husband had been in adultery with his wife. I remember an incredible calm coming over me, I think because I knew that this was God's answer to my prayer the night before, and He had prepared my heart for such a time as this.

My husband had seen the name on the caller ID and thought I was going to ask him to leave, as I had done before. Instead, I asked him to sit down with me and I told him I forgave him!! He cried, told me how sorry he was, and said he could not believe that I could forgive him for what he had done. It had to be God's very own mercy flowing through me, because it was real and something I could never have manufactured myself, even if I had wanted to! I didn't have to "will" myself to say anything—the words just came out, gracious and loving and merciful. The other reason I know that it was from the Lord is because it was permanent! Although I've had to extend forgiveness for other things, I have not had to continue to "re-forgive" my husband for that morning or anything leading up to it.

I became pregnant the same day my husband began his relationship with the OW. My husband says now that it was probably no accident that I miscarried the same week he ended it (which was before I found out what was going on); he truly felt that the loss of our child was a punishment for his sin. However, not only did God graciously allow me to "miss" all of the signs of the OW during that time, but He blessed me amazingly through a pregnancy that lasted only ten weeks! I was given the gift of delivering, seeing, holding, and burying our tiny baby, perfectly formed and the size of my thumb! God used the same event that seared my husband's conscience to bless me (Titus 1:15).

In just a few short weeks, that little person was already fulfilling the purpose God had planned for him since before the beginning of time, and God granted me favor by allowing me to carry that sweet child who is at this very moment in the presence of Jesus! God showed me His incredible mercy and forgiveness during that time, not only for my sin of having children out of wedlock but also for the sin of aborting His perfect creations before they were born. Although I knew I was already forgiven, He blessed me by letting me see this perfect baby and showed me that I not only have a whole "family" of children in His presence at this very moment, but in fact they are already waiting to greet me whenever He takes me home! I am amazed and humbled at God's mercy—that He would forgive me so completely that I can now rejoice at this fact with tears of hope and joy instead of tears of mourning!

I don't know for sure—His ways are so much higher than my ways—but to have experienced God's mercy so completely during that time may also have prepared my heart so that I could offer that same tender love and mercy to my husband.

The amazing thing is that when God allowed me to forgive my husband, He also turned my husband's heart so that he forgave me for all of my sins against him both before and during our marriage! That alone made the entire trial worthwhile! I truly believe there is great power in forgiveness—and, as I learned through RMI, there is not much that is more alluring!

We had a wonderful month after what I would now call our "restoration." We went away for a long weekend with our boys and it truly felt like the honeymoon we never had! As if confirming God's will for our marriage, a woman who didn't even know us approached me at the hot springs and told me what a beautiful family we had—she said that she could "tell" that there was truly something special in our marriage! God was beginning to show me that He had plans to fulfill the "desires of my heart" for my husband and our family.

I would like to be able to tell you that our trial stopped there and we lived happily ever after, but unfortunately things again took a turn for the worse. Everyone, even many of my Christian friends, began to tell me that I couldn't possibly forgive "so easily," that we would surely have to "talk about" and "work through our issues" or our marriage would never "really get better." Can you believe that after all that God had shown me about the dangers (and futility) of psychology and counseling (Isa. 30:1–3, Jer. 8:22, Isa. 5:13), I still took the bait?!! Within six weeks, after being told by our pastors that we should see a "professional counselor" instead of meeting with them (our first choice), we were back in counseling, dredging up the past and venting our feelings (Prov. 29:11, Phil. 3:13–14) instead of rejoicing in what God had done.

I even saw the old counselor one time (who I later discovered was going through a divorce herself) and took her advice to chat with another woman whose husband was unfaithful. After talking to these two women, I insisted that my husband take a lie detector test to "prove" that the OW was really out of the picture! Since my husband was eager to do anything to please me, he agreed. Immediately afterward, God impressed upon me the verse "some trust in horses and chariots, but we trust in the Lord our God" (Ps. 20:7). I realized that not only had I let my husband down by my ridiculous demands, but, even worse, I had let God down by placing my trust not in Him alone but in physical "evidence" I could see (which He certainly controlled anyway—Prov. 16:33—but that possibility escaped me at the time). I know, I know—you'd think I would have figured out by now that "friendship with the world is hostility toward God"! But I am foolish and stubborn and it takes me longer than most.... Praise God that He is patient and never gives up!

After a few months of counseling, by God's grace, my husband had the wisdom to see that we were going nowhere, always looking into ourselves instead of at God. On top of that, we were sick at the money we had to spend to get "advice" from those who were "peddling the Word of God," when the Mighty Counselor gives His counsel and wisdom freely to all who ask!! How much wiser would I have been had

I gone to Him alone in the first place, and had I looked to older women to guide me in how to be a godly wife!

About that time, by God's divine providence, I "happened to" stumble across the Restore Ministries website, unexpectedly and out of the blue! I ordered the resources, including the Wise Woman workbook, which completely convicted me of all I was still doing wrong. I set to work to begin doing all of the things that I had never known about before! I was completely convicted of my contentiousness and asked God to help me stop arguing. I began to treat my husband as the spiritual leader of our home, deferring to him in everything he asked, and even insisting that my teenage girls do so also. ("What is wrong with you, Mom? Why don't you stand up for yourself?!" They thought I had gone off the deep end.)

I had never thought much about the verse that God turns the king's heart like channels of water (Prov. 21:1), but once I got a hold of that, everything changed! I also praised and thanked God that Erin showed me that God is the head of Christ, and "Christ is the head of EVERY man" (1 Cor. 11:3)! Knowing those two verses, I began to take everything to God in prayer, and what a difference it made! When I took my concerns to God first, He began to turn my husband's heart on specific issues without my ever saying a word!! He even began to turn my husband's heart toward me, with a tenderness and sweetness that I didn't know he still had!

(At one point, I suggested that home schooling my eighth grade daughter might be the answer to some issues she was having at school. Her dad said no, my husband said no, and she insisted she would run away from home if I tried. I didn't say another word to anyone but took it to God in prayer. Within three days, all three of them had changed their minds and all came to me, asking me to home school her for a season!)

I give all praise and glory to God for how He is changing me and drawing me closer to Himself. I praise Him for His Word ("Thy Word is Truth," John 17:17) and thank Him that He equipped Erin to painstakingly take the time to pull together all of the Scriptures about being a godly wife and mother—it is truly a blessing to have them all right at hand when a trial comes! I praise Him for Erin's unwavering commitment to speaking the Truth in love, and for not ever compromising or watering down God's Word. I am a living testimony to the fact that God wants us to trust completely in Him—without any doubting, double mindedness, or friendship with the world. It is only when I trust in God alone that I can truly say, "The joy of the Lord is my strength"!

Yes, Jesus demands radical obedience, but where else would I go if not to Him (John 6:68)—He has the words of eternal life! I praise Him for His infinite grace and mercy when I fall short; He enables me to keep getting back up, and His mercies are new every morning! I can trust that He will complete every good work He has begun, and His grace is sufficient for me.

I must admit, it's a bit scary to write all of this down and put it "out there" for others to read, but I pray that what I write will give hope to others that He can forgive ANY sin, and that they would know how wide and long and high and deep is the love and forgiveness of Christ. "This is a faithful saying and worthy of all acceptance, that Christ Jesus came into the world to save sinners, of whom I am chief" (1 Tim. 1:15).

Most of all, I praise Him for the shed blood of Jesus, which covers my sins and enables me to have a relationship with my Maker and Creator! Nothing compares to the unspeakable joy of knowing Him, of sitting at the feet of Jesus and learning from Him. To me, He alone is the pearl of great price, worth any cost!

Chapter 37

Melanie

"So when they were filled,
He said to His disciples,
'Gather up the fragments that remain,
so that nothing is lost.'"
—John 6:12

"Look to GOD!"

I suffered (or so I thought) the worst marriage for almost five years. I could not see anything except that God had put my husband and me together just to torture each other. Everything about my husband made me sick. I had no love anymore for him, couldn't stand to be around him, and especially couldn't stand to be intimate.

I finally got so fed up that I started seeking a way out of the marriage, for I knew that God hates divorce. I searched for Scriptures and even sought for approval from other Christians.

One night as I was searching the Word, I asked the Lord for a sign and for my husband to come home and not start with me for no reason at all (as usual). I told the Lord that if he came home and started an argument, that would be the sign, as if it were okay for me to go ahead and file for a divorce the following day.

So guess what happened? Yep!! He came home and started with me, and that was all I needed to make me feel good about what I was planning to do. So I filed, had him put out by the police, and had him served papers. I hurt deeply inside because I knew then that I really did love him but hated his ways.

He immediately told me that he could not live in the same state with me. He left for Florida but called every day wanting to come back home. He even agreed to go to counseling.

On the following Monday, I called to put the divorce on hold and agreed to go to counseling, but would not let my husband come back home because I didn't see the changes that I thought were good enough. Counseling was a mess!! The counselor pretty much kicked us out. He told us that if we could not commit to each other and tell each other that we were both willing to try and give our best, then there was no reason to come back to his office.

WOW!! That was pretty harsh, and I didn't even care. By this time my heart was even harder than it had ever been before. What is worse, I am saved, sanctified, and Holy Ghost filled!! I am the Praise and Worship Leader at my church but could not get my marriage together!! How is that for HOLY?!!

My husband got called up on active duty with the National Guard and, even though his unit didn't have to go out of the country, they had to serve as security for about a year at another army unit. This distance caused him to slide even further back from the Lord, because he didn't have strong support from other men.

After about a year, God started dealing with me about my marriage. I needed to get this thing together!! At the beginning of the year, I started praying for our marriage and for God to change me.

As I finally began to really want my marriage, my husband had changed his mind and now wanted a divorce! I wanted him to come home, but he did not want to anymore. I just couldn't understand.

One night I was searching the web for restored marriage testimonies. I clicked on the RMI link and read the intro. Talk about God speaking!! I felt like I had hit the jackpot! I truly could see this as a sign that God was going to restore our marriage. I immediately ordered the Resource Packet and joined the fellowship!! I could hardly wait to receive my packet! I was like a child with a brand new toy! I immediately started reading and eating the words!

It was as I began to seek the Lord and stand in the gap that I found out about the so-called OW (other woman)—one for whom my husband bought a cell phone and that I was never supposed to know about. I really relied on RMI and my ePartner. The first ePartner I got did not respond to my email, so I immediately got discouraged. But then I sent another request and was blessed to have found a true friend!! I thank God for her because she prayed for (and with me), which helped me through all my fears and kept me encouraged.

She put a lot of things in perspective and helped me conquer that test!! This was so painful, especially now, because God had started breaking me and showing me how to forgive, filling me with His unconditional love. Love that loves even in the worst situation. Even in sin! My heart was pierced with indescribable pain! I cried for days and couldn't eat but was constantly in prayer. I soon began to realize that God was purifying me! It was painful but very well worth it!!

Every time I thought about the cell phone, which he purchased with a contract, or it would ring, I got mad. I constantly let the devil defeat me with that cell phone! All I could see was that he was divorcing me and was going to go be with her. By this time my husband was constantly telling me that he was back to be with me and to stop worrying about something that I couldn't change. (His telling me that did not help me; he could have been lying for all I knew.)

One morning while praying (before I found RMI), the Spirit told me to go to 1 Peter 3:1: "In the same way, you wives, be submissive to your own husbands so that even if any of them are disobedient to the word, they may be won without a word by the behavior of their wives." As I read, I knew what it was saying but at the same time I didn't. I asked God over and over, "What does this mean?" Then, as I started reading my resources, and there it was!!!

Learning to say "not a word" was so hard! Yes, I failed that test many times!! (Thank You, Lord, for being so forgiving.) I also learned what it really means to be in subjection and submissive to my husband. My hardest test was being submissive and obedient while there was a divorce pending, and knowing about the OW.

When my husband told me that he did not see us being able to start over unless we got a divorce first, God showed me that He was in control and we would start over without a divorce. God showed me that my husband's heart was truly in His hands and He would turn it sooner than I would think!

After finding RMI and my constantly seeking the Lord, my husband and I grew closer and closer. We spent everyday together. God showed me His power in many, many situations.

God had given me so many confirmations that He had already restored my marriage and, even with a divorce hearing scheduled for May, I had no doubt that God was going to restore our marriage. I was full of faith. My ePartner was full of faith. One of my closest friends at work was full of faith. All we were waiting for was the manifestation—the true sign: the divorce cancellation!!

On Sunday, my husband told me that he loved me!! PTL!!

And then on Thursday, he spoke the words that I had been waiting to hear: "I am not going to go through with the divorce." PTL!! Hallelujah!

On Mother's Day, he gave me back my original wedding rings, which I had declared I would never wear again and said that, if he wanted me back, he would have to buy me a new set. When I saw those rings, they were new enough for me. He even put them on my finger himself. He has moved back home and that in itself is WONDERFUL, because he had told me that he did not want to come back to this same apartment. But look at GOD....

I encourage everyone to hold onto every promise of the Lord, for He is faithful and will do exceedingly abundantly above all that you could ask or even just think about! Trust me—I know! Don't give up—the end result is so much worth the wait and even the pain!!

All the resources are wonderful but I truly found the How God Can and Will Restore Your Marriage and A Wise Woman to be the most helpful! They immediately made me see myself and caused me to repent for many, many things, and many, many times.

I truly thank God because even when my ePartner saw the signs of restoration, she did not get jealous—she just prayed even harder for the complete restoration and manifestation of restoration. I love you, Laura, a dear friend for life!! God has promised you restoration and He will do just what He said!! Get ready, get ready, get ready! Your blessing is coming!!

What you have read is just a *small sample* of the POWER and FAITHFULNESS of God that are told through countless restored marriages! We continue to post new restored marriage, and restored relationship testimonies (children, siblings, parents, etc.) on our site each week.

Don't let ANYONE try to convince you that God cannot restore YOUR marriage! It is a lie. The TRUTH is that He is MORE THAN ABLE!!

Is Your Marriage... Crumbling? Hopeless? Or Ended in Divorce?

At Last There's Hope!

Have you been searching for marriage help online? It's not by chance, nor is it by coincidence, that you have this book in your hands. God is leading you to Restore Ministries that began by helping marriages that *appear* hopeless—like yours!

God has heard your cry for help in your marriage struggles and defeats. He predestined this **Divine Appointment** to give you the hope that you so desperately need right now!

We know and understand what you are going through since many of us in our restoration fellowship have a restored marriage and family! No matter what others have told you, your marriage is not hopeless! We know, after filling almost two books of restored marriage testimonies, that God is able to restore any marriage—especially yours!

"Behold, I am the LORD, the God of all flesh; is anything too difficult for Me?" (Jeremiah 32:27).

If you have been told that your marriage is hopeless or that without your husband's help your marriage cannot be restored! Each week we post a new Restored Relationship from one of our Restoration Fellowship Members that we post on our site.

"Ah Lord GOD! Behold, You have made the heavens and the earth by Your great power and by Your outstretched arm! Nothing is too difficult for You"! (Jeremiah 32:17).

If you have been crying out to God for more help, someone who understands, someone you can talk to, then we invite you to join our RMI Restoration Fellowship. Since beginning this fellowship, we have seen more marriages restored on a regular basis than we ever thought possible!

Restoration Fellowship

Restoration is a "narrow road"—look around, most marriages end in divorce! But if your desire is for a restored marriage, then our Restoration Fellowship is designed especially for you!

Since beginning this fellowship, we have seen marriages restored more consistently than we ever thought possible.

Let us help you stay committed to "working with God" to restore your marriages. Restoration Fellowship can offer you the help, guidance, and support you will need to stay on the path that leads to victory— *your* marriage restored!

Let us assure you that all of our marriages were restored by GOD (through His Word) as we sought Him to lead us, teach us, guide us and transform us through His Holy Spirit. This, too, is all you need for *your* marriage to be restored.

However, God continues to lead people to our ministry and fellowship to gain the faith, support and help that so many say that they needed in their time of crisis.

"Thank GOD for this ministry. Without it, I know the principles taught to me saved me from completely destroying my marriage. I had so many well-intentioned Christians tell me to use tough love and get what I "deserve" when it comes to the divorce. They encouraged me by saying things like "God knows you didn't do anything wrong, He is going to make sure you are well taken care of". Well, they weren't entirely wrong. He has taken very good care of me, but I did do a lot wrong. And learned He loves and forgives me anyway. Thank you so much for being honest! The truth was very foreign to me at first, and some of the principles were off-putting. I didn't want to think of Him as my Heavenly Husband. "That's weird," I thought, but the more I grew in love with Him, the less awkward and weird it became. It made sense and I rejoice in the fact that He will always take care of me as His bride." Maria in Illinois

"I must say I would definitely recommend the book How God Can and Will Restore Your Marriage to other women who have never married because it provides educational truth and tools needed to grow in our relationships with the Lord and brings to our attention how we need to

let God be God and let Him make changes in us so that we can be the godly wife, mother, and women that we need to be and to leave our crisis in God's hands." Lorena, who has **never married**

"Thank you so much for spending time and believing that GOD will and can restore our marriages no matter what our circumstance is. When I came across this website I was a total mess. THIS ministry encouraged me more than words can ever say, taking a course day by day really got me through these last 2 months." Damaris in Texas

Join our Restoration Fellowship TODAY and allow us to help YOU **restore** YOUR marriage.

Like What You've Read?

If you've been blessed by this book
get the full WOTT Series available
on EncouragingBookstore.com & Amazon.com

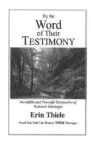

By the Word of Their Testimony (Book 1): Incredible and Powerful Testimonies of Restored Marriages

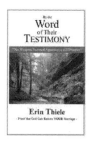

By the Word of Their Testimony (Book 2): No Weapon Formed Against you will Prosper

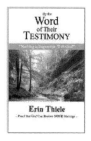

By the Word of Their Testimony (Book 3): Nothing is Impossible With God

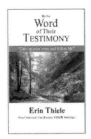

Word of Their Testimony (Book 4): Take up your cross and follow Me

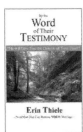

Word of Their Testimony (Book 5): He will Give You the Desires of Your Heart

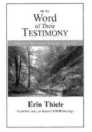

Word of Their Testimony (Book 6): Proclaim the Good News to Everyone

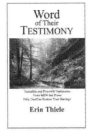

Word of Their Testimony: Incredible and Powerful Testimonies of Restored Marriages From Men

Mentioned in this Book

Also available
on EncouragingBookstore.com & Amazon.com

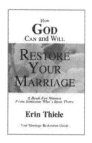

How God Can and Will Restore Your Marriage:
From Someone Who's Been There

A Wise Woman: A Wise Woman Builds Her House
By a FOOL Who First Built on Sinking Sand

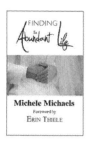

Finding the Abundant Life by Michele Michaels

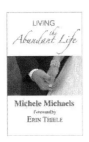 Living the Abundant Life by Michele Michaels

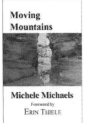 Moving Mountains by Michele Michaels

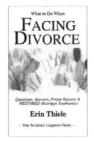 What to Do When Facing Divorce

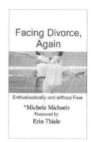

Facing Divorce —Again by Michele Michaels

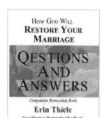

Questions and Answers: How God Will Restore Your Marriage

Restore Ministries International

POB 830 Ozark, MO 65721 USA

For more help
Please visit one of our Websites:

EncouragingWomen.org

HopeAtLast.com

RestoreMinistries.net

RMIEW.com

Aidemaritale.com (French)

AjudaMatrimonial.com (Portuguese)

AyudaMatrimonial.com (Spanish)

Pag-asa.org (Tagalog Filipino)

Uiteindelikhoop.com (Afrikaans)

Zachranamanzelstva.com (Slovakian)

EncouragingMen.org

Where you'll also find FREE Courses for men and women.

Made in the USA
Middletown, DE
28 February 2023

25828908R00115